KU-216-460

Travellers

CANARY ISLANDS

BY
PAUL MURPHY

Produced by
Thomas Cook Publishing

Written by Paul Murphy

Original photography by Clive Sawyer

Edited and designed by Laburnum
Technologies Pvt Ltd, C-533 Triveni Apts,
Sheikh Sarai Phase 1, New Delhi 110017

Published by Thomas Cook Publishing
A division of Thomas Cook Holdings Ltd

PO Box 227, The Thomas Cook Business
Park, Units 19–21, Coningsby Road,
Peterborough PE3 8XX, United Kingdom
E-mail: books@thomascook.com
www.thomascookpublishing.com

ISBN: 1-841572-35-7

Text © 2002 Thomas Cook Publishing
Maps © 2002 Thomas Cook Publishing
First edition © 2002 Thomas Cook Publishing

Managing Director: Kevin Fitzgerald

Publisher: Donald Greig

Series Consultant: Vivien Stone

All rights reserved. No part of this publication may be reproduced,
stored in a retrieval system or transmitted, in any form or by any means,
electronic, mechanical, recording or otherwise, in any part of the world,
without prior permission of the publisher. Requests for permission
should be addressed to Thomas Cook Publishing, PO Box 227,
The Thomas Cook Business Park, Units 19–21, Coningsby Road,
Peterborough, PE3 8XX, United Kingdom.

Although every care has been taken in compiling this publication, and
the contents are believed to be correct at the time of printing, Thomas
Cook Holdings Ltd cannot accept any responsibility for errors or
omissions, however caused, or for changes in details given in the
guidebook, or for the consequences of any reliance on the information
provided.

The opinions and assessments expressed in this book do not necessarily
represent those of Thomas Cook Holdings Ltd.

Printed and bound in Spain by: Grafo Industrias Gráficas, Basauri

Cover: Strelitzias (Bird of Paradise). Photograph by Clive Sawyer.
Inside cover: photographs supplied by Spectrum Colour Library

CD manufacturing services provided by business interactive ltd, Rutland, UK

Contents

Introduction

The Canary Islands were born as an international holiday playground in the late 1950s. Since then they have entered the north European psyche as a synonym for winter sunshine. In the year 2000 alone, the islands welcomed over ten million visitors.

The fishing port of Puerto de la Cruz

Despite its popularity, however, few people have any real knowledge of the archipelago. Even naming the seven islands, beyond Gran Canaria, Tenerife, and Lanzarote, would be difficult for most. The Canaries are popular precisely because they provide great numbers of people with simple 'sun and fun' holidays, and this has led to some resorts being transformed into concrete jungles and pastiches of home-life culture. Yet, to typecast the whole of a diverse island group on the evidence of two or three of its resorts is as ridiculous as writing off all Spain for a deviant *costa* or two. Beyond the beaches there is much to be commended by even the sternest travel critic. The scenery on all these volcanic islands is spectacular: from soft green valleys to charred lunarscapes, from Arizona-like gorges to snowy peaks and Sahara-scale sand dunes. Four out of the ten Spanish national parks are concentrated in this relatively tiny archipelago, giving the lie to anyone who believes nature always comes second to tourism here.

Canary Islands

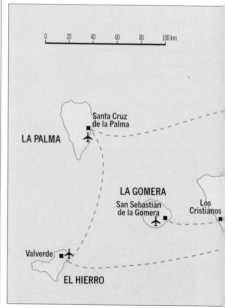

*These islands enjoy a fortunate climate . . . they offer
not only good rich soil . . . but also wild fruits to nourish people
without work or effort . . . these are the
Elysian fields of which Homer sang.*

PLUTARCH

Life of Sertorius 1st–2nd century AD

Cultural, historical, and ethnic features are admittedly limited, but there is more than enough to occupy the average two-week stay. Caves of the original aboriginal inhabitants lie open to discovery, the cities have fine museums and galleries, and there are superb examples of Spanish Colonial architecture in towns untouched by tourism. Folk traditions and island heritage are also still very much alive – to see *Canarios* at their best, just catch a fiesta.

It's quite easy to sample the 'real' Canaries. Just get off the beach, drive away from the resorts, and look around you. You'll be pleasantly surprised at what lies beyond.

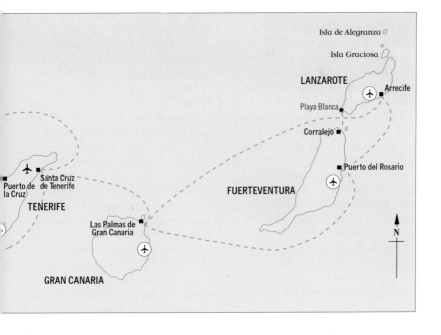

The Land

The Canary Islands comprise seven major and six very small islands, situated between 96km and 304km off the northwest coast of North Africa. Some 496km lie between the easternmost island (Lanzarote) and the westernmost island (El Hierro). The next stop west of El Hierro is the Americas.

Striated rock formations at Los Gigantes, Tenerife

For historical reasons the Canaries are Spanish territory, although the southern coast of Spain lies 1,120km to the north. Geographically, the Canaries actually belong to a larger island grouping known as Macaronesia (Blessed Islands), which comprises the Azores, Madeira, and Cape Verde islands. All of these volcanic islands have topographical and fauna and flora features in common.

Landscapes and Statistics

Each island is of volcanic origin and is dotted with volcanic cones, either long extinct and overgrown, or quite bare and, on Lanzarote and La Palma, still smouldering (*see pp8–9*).

The largest of the islands is Tenerife, with an area of 2,057sq km, and a population of approximately 685,000. It is dominated by Mount Teide, at 3,718m the highest mountain on Spanish territory. The island's mountainous northeast and northwest corners are lush, while its southern shores are parched and arid.

The next largest island is Fuerteventura, which has an area of 1,731sq km. With a population of only around 42,350, however, it has the the lowest density amongst the islands.

Fuerteventura is also the oldest and, topographically, the least dramatic island, many of its volcanoes reduced to mere hummocks by the erosion of 20 million years. It is almost barren.

Gran Canaria covers a similar-sized area to Fuerteventura – 1,532sq km – and has the highest and most densely packed population (approximately 733,600) of any of the islands, two-thirds of whom live in Las Palmas. Gran Canaria is a classic volcanic cone in profile, with a series of mountains climbing towards a central peak of 1,949m (Pico de las Nieves). The north of the island is wetter, cooler, and greener than the arid south.

Lanzarote and La Palma are similar in both size – 795sq km and 728sq km respectively – and population (around 79,400 and 82,000). The south of Lanzarote is also very dry. It was devastated by 18th-century eruptions which have left a fantastic, lunar-like landscape. The north is comparatively green and mountainous.

La Palma has a great central ridge (*cumbre*) running north–south along its length, culminating in a massive mature crater or *caldera* (*see pp8–9*). It is by far the greenest of all the islands, and the only place (aside from Tenerife's Barranco del Infierno) where running water can regularly be found.

At 378sq km, La Gomera is around half the size of Lanzarote and La Palma, inhabited by just 16,350 people. Like Gran Canaria, it is a dome-shaped island and also has a north–south weather divide. At the centre is a plateau, almost continually covered in mist, with a dense laurel forest.

Last and least is El Hierro, covering 277sq km, with a population of just 8,500. It is a semi-circular sweeping curve of an island. Were the sea to be rolled back and the circle completed, a huge collapsed volcanic crater would be revealed. The landscape is green and varied, though not as dramatic as the other western islands. (*See also pp138–9 for details of the six tiny islets off Lanzarote and Fuerteventura.*)

Volcanic Mount Teide seen from Las Rosas, La Gomera

All the Canaries are volcanic islands, typically formed when molten rock and ash force their way up through the earth's core and the seabed to form a cone-shaped island, often scored by deep gullies (*barrancos*).

The first island to be born was Fuerteventura, some 20 million years ago; Lanzarote appeared about four million years later, followed by Gran Canaria after another two to three million years. The rest of the group emerged over the course of the next 13 million years.

The nature of the volcanic scenery on each island depends how recent and how extensive the eruptions were, and on the forces of erosion and nature's reclamation of the land. There are few places in the world as spectacular as the fantastic 'moonscapes' of Tenerife and Lanzarote (only Hawaii and Iceland are comparable). Here, cataclysmic events occurred very recently in geographical terms.

Mount Teide was blowing as Columbus passed in 1492, and there were further sizeable eruptions in 1604, 1605, 1704–5, 1706, 1798, and 1909.

The south of Lanzarote was devastated between 1730 and 1736, and suffered again from 1812 to 1824. The most recent eruptions occurred on La Palma, in 1949 and 1971. These were slight compared with earlier occasions; the explosion that formed the island's Caldera de Taburiente, some 400,000 years ago, was enormous – it is from here that the word *caldera* (volcanic crater) actually originates.

As you tour the *malpais* (badlands) caused by the eruptions, you can see the three main types of volcanic debris: *picon* or *lapilli* – the tiny, light cinder particles put to good effect by Canarian farmers *(see pp74–5)*; pumice or *escoria*

pahoe-pahoe (the Hawaiian term for rope lava). The slower moving debris, which cools into slab-like folds, is known as pillow lava.

Geologists will have a field day wandering the Cañadas del Teide *(see pp90–91)* identifying the various volcanic rock types. But if you simply want to be entertained, see how Lanzarote designer César Manrique made both a home and tourist attractions from the underground passages formed by the molten lava, and visit the Cueva de los Verdes on Lanzarote. Above all, you should not miss a trip to Lanzarote's Montañas del Fuego, first by coach, then on foot *(see pp70–71 and pp80–81)*.

– small, lightweight, honeycombed rocks produced by the formation of gas bubbles in slow-flowing lava; and volcanic 'bombs' – heavy, solid rocks, sometimes as big as footballs, with a brittle outer coat.

The lava, too, comes in distinct types. If it is the fast-flowing variety, it cools into rope-like coils and is known as

The most spectacular 'badlands' are to be found on Tenerife (far left and above) and Lanzarote (centre)

History and Governance

In 1982 the Canary Islands were granted autonomy (the right to self-government) as part of the general Spanish policy of decentralisation. Their government is conducted jointly from the two capitals of Las Palmas de Gran Canaria (for the eastern islands) and Santa Cruz de Tenerife (for the western islands). Las Palmas has been assigned half of the regional government departments and the islands' Supreme Court, while Santa Cruz has the other half of the departments and the Parliament. Each of the two provinces has a governor appointed by Madrid.

Statuesque reminder of the ancient Guanches

1st–2nd century BC	The Canaries are settled by a tribe with both Cro-Magnon and Mediterranean features, probably of Berber origin from North Africa and subsequently called Guanches (*see pp14–15*).
25 BC–AD 23	Ships arrive from the Roman colony of Mauritania, find native dogs, and name the islands (*see p24*).
1st–2nd century AD	The Roman writer, Pliny the Elder, mentions the islands for the first time in his *Natural History*, calling them the Fortunate Isles. The islands are mapped by the Greek geographer, Ptolemy, who recognises El Hierro as the westernmost point of the known world.
Around 1312	Genoese seafarer, Lanzalotto Malocello, lands on the island of Tytheroygatra. His motives and actions are unclear, but the island is later renamed Lanzarote.
1339–42	The first mention of Isla Canaria appears on maps. Spanish vessels are launched in search of the islands, though no conquests are recorded.
Late 14th–early 15th centuries	The Canaries come increasingly to the notice of European slave-traders and treasure-hunters. In 1402, the Norman baron, Jean de

Béthencourt, with the help of Spanish nobleman Gadifer de la Salle, sails under the flag of Henry III of Castile, intending to capture Gran Canaria and Tenerife. Instead, he occupies Lanzarote and begins colonisation.

1404–06 Using Lanzarote as a staging post for reinforcements, Béthencourt sails to Fuerteventura and, within a year, succeeds in subduing the island. He then turns his attentions to El Hierro, where he tricks the small population into slavery. However, he meets strong armed resistance on La Gomera, Gran Canaria, and La Palma and returns to France.

1478–88 Ferdinand and Isabella of Spain order the second phase of the Conquest. A force led by Juan Réjon lands on Gran Canaria and founds Las Palmas. After five years of bitter fighting, Gran Canaria is captured. After another five years, La Gomera is also subdued.

1492 Christopher Columbus uses the islands as a final staging post before his voyage to the New World (*see pp36–7*).

The Guanches' sacred Roque Nublo above Tejeda on Gran Canaria

1493	Alonso Fernández de Lugo lands on La Palma and completes its capture by stealth, tricking the last resisting chieftain into captivity.
1494	De Lugo's forces on Tenerife are routed in the Orotava Valley. But de Lugo returns to the valley with reinforcements and, following a bloody battle, the site is proclaimed La Victoria (Victory) in honour of the last battle of the Conquest.
16th–17th century	The islands use slave labour to gain economic wealth, first from sugar, then from wine.
Early 19th century	Cochineal, a red dye extracted from cactus-feeding insects, becomes the new island industry. This lasts until the advent of chemical dyes elsewhere in the world in the 1870s. Its collapse leads to large-scale emigration to South America.
1852	In order to stimulate the Canarian economy, Santa Cruz de Tenerife and Las Palmas de Gran Canaria are declared free-trade zones by Queen Isabella II, and become two of the world's busiest ports.
1880s	The first Canarian bananas are exported and become a mainstay of the islands' economy.
1936	General Francisco Franco, mistrusted by the Spanish government, is posted to Tenerife where he plans the military coup leading to the Spanish Civil War (1936–9). The islands quickly fall to his forces.
1960s	Tenerife and Gran Canaria embrace package tourism.
1971	The most recent volcanic eruption on the islands occurs on La Palma.
1982	The Canaries are made an autonomous region under the new post-Franco constitution.
1989	The Canary Islands, as part of Spain, become full members of the European Community.
21st century	Rapidly developing infrastructure expands the tourism industry.

Government offices in Plaza de España

Representation and Structure

The Canarian Parliament comprises 15 members from Gran Canaria, 15 members from Tenerife, eight from La Palma, eight from Lanzarote, seven from Fuerteventura, four from La Gomera, and three from El Hierro.

In addition to its legislative role, the parliament sets island budgets and appoints representatives to present its case to the mainland.

Each island also has its own island council, known as the *Cabildo Insular*, which possesses certain powers of self-government and accepts responsibility for local services. These functions are in turn delegated to *municipios* (regional municipal units), then to town authorities, whose *ayuntamiento* (town hall) is usually a handsome traditional building in the central square.

The Independence Movement

The most obvious sign of Canarian discontent with the mainland is roadside graffiti spelling 'Spanish Go Home' or 'Godos Out'.

'Godos' (literally meaning 'Goths') refers to Spanish island workers, convenient scapegoats accused of taking jobs which should rightly belong to the locals. This does, of course, happen in some cases, but the 'Godos' also provide skills lost in previous bouts of emigration, when many able islanders went to South America in search of a better future.

The main party is the Coalición Canaria (CC), which carries around one-third of the popular vote. Its aims are moderate, directed more towards greater autonomy than towards full independence.

The Guanches

The term 'Guanche' meant 'native of Tenerife' in the original island language, but was subsequently used as a name for all the islanders who occupied the archipelago before the Spanish Conquest in the 15th century.

The Guanches almost certainly came from North Africa in the 1st or 2nd century BC, probably fleeing persecution, possibly in primitive boats. Little is known about their origins, and new theories and discoveries are frequently advanced. In appearance they were fair-skinned and sometimes blue-eyed and blond-haired (the Arabs did not colonise North Africa until much later).

There are no written records of the Guanches until the medieval voyages of Malocello (see p10) and the Spanish conquistadores. The Spanish discovered a people still living in the Stone Age: metals were unknown to them, and many Guanches still lived in caves, both natural and man-made. They were by no means savages, however. Some of the earliest Spanish journals praise them highly for their morality, courage, and intelligence.

The best indicators of Guanche life have been found in their tombs. Like the ancient Egyptians, they ritually embalmed their dead, and mummies and other finds are on display at the archaeological museums in Santa Cruz de Tenerife and Las Palmas de Gran Canaria. They also appear to have had a cryptic language of symbols, evidence of which has been found carved on rocks. So few have survived, however, that translation is extremely difficult.

When the Spanish arrived, most islands were divided into several chiefdoms or kingdoms (menceyatos), each ruled by a mencey who was advised by a council of elderly men. As elsewhere in the New World, the Spanish pursued a policy of divide and rule, making alliances with friendly kings, and encouraging Guanche to fight Guanche, until resistance was quelled. Aside from set-piece battles, however, the body count on both sides appears to have been relatively low, and the inadvertent import of European diseases probably killed more Guanches than did battle.

Life on the post-conquest islands varied. Many Guanches were enslaved; collaborators were well treated; a minority inter-married, and many were simply ignored by the new colonists. A significant number remained in hiding in the mountains, but many Guanches were coerced and intimidated by the Spanish Inquisition into 'abandoning their roots'.

Within a few decades, it is estimated that two-thirds of the indigenous people had disappeared, and within a century or so this ancient society had all but vanished.

Reminders of a lost culture – statues of the Guanche people at Candelaria, Tenerife (left), and Doramas Park, Las Palmas, Gran Canaria

Culture

The Canary Islands are a pot-pourri of many different cultures. On the larger islands you will find field workers and resort workers, cave-dwellers and city-dwellers, all within a few kilometres of each other. Yet many Canarios have never even left their islands, and the difference between Las Palmas and El Hierro is mind-boggling. What, then, is the cultural bond (if indeed, there is such a thing) that holds this fragmented society together?

On the larger islands a touristy ambience prevails

Guanche Culture

The Guanche language, dress, religion, and other habits were extinguished by the *conquistadores* long ago (*see pp14–15*). Judging by the poor state of repair that Guanche sites are found in today, modern Canarios seem to have no great interest in their ancestors. This may partly be due to the absence of information about the first islanders, or may be because of Franco's policy of destroying any trace of pre-Spanish history on the islands, which makes it almost impossible to draw up a true picture of their society. There are still cave-dwellers today (at Chinamada on Tenerife, for example), but they probably have virtually nothing in common with their forebears.

Spanish Culture

The islanders may speak Spanish and look Spanish, but does this make them Spanish? A Las Palmas banker may say yes, a Lanzarote farmer may say no. For many years, particularly under the Franco regime, the islands were 'the forgotten Spain' (as were many

mainland rural regions). This feeling of 'the poor relations' was graphically illustrated, until quite recently, by the fact that Canarian TV screens would go blank during Spanish television commercial breaks; advertisers simply didn't think it was worth showing their products to the impoverished islanders. The new wealth of tourism has changed that way of thinking.

Canarian separatism is often mooted and is the subject of popular graffiti, but true independence (as opposed to autonomy, which the islands do enjoy) is not really on the nation's agenda. This situation is happily accepted by the Canarian banana-growers, who sell over 90 per cent of their crop to mainland Spain.

The popular images of Spanish culture, such as bullfighting and flamenco dancing, mean nothing to Canarios (the latter is staged only for tourists). Spanish *joie de vivre* at fiesta time is well embraced, however, and the Carnival celebrations on Tenerife are said to be the best outside Rio de Janeiro and New Orleans. This is also a chance for the island's South American cultural influence to emerge (*see pp11–12*). Café life (*see pp160–61*), the siesta, and football fervour are other shared Spanish passions.

Inter-island Rivalry

The two capitals of Las Palmas and Santa Cruz de Tenerife are forever competing to offer the best banks, the best port, the best cultural facilities, and so on. For example, Las Palmas had to win a fierce battle for a second Canarian University to compete with that of La Laguna on Tenerife. The other islands are regarded as backwaters, and La Gomera, in particular, is frequently the butt of jokes.

New Influences

Tourism has inevitably had a major effect on many islanders. While those with businesses in the new resorts of Playa de Las Américas and Maspalomas have prospered and become the *nouveau riche*, many more islanders have been left behind. Youngsters have swapped a life of drudgery in the fields for working for low wages in foreign-owned hotels, while their communities, starved of new blood, slowly die. This is surely the worst

of both worlds. Others, keen to develop their own communities to attract tourists, are either knowingly or unwittingly bulldozing their own heritage. Conservationists are seeking to redress this balance and re-educate the people (as César Manrique did on Lanzarote in his lifetime). They have proved that it is possible to combine local pride, character, and integrity with profitable tourism. These are exciting times for the Canarios. Money and adventure beckon, but family roots and village loyalties are still strong.

Tenerife costume, here modelled by folk dancers, echoes the vivid island flora

Fiestas

Canarians love to let their hair down. In fact, to the visitor, it sometimes seems that island life is just one big round of parties – religious holidays, island patron saint days, village saint days, city foundation days, a day to celebrate the repulse of an English pirate attack, a day to mark the miraculous discovery of an image of the Virgin, and so on. Add to this the largest annual jamboree, the two-week *Carnaval*, and it's a fair bet that some time during your holiday you will bump into at least one fiesta.

BAJADAS

Aside from the *Bajada de la Rama* at Agaete, there are two other very important *bajadas* ('descents'). On La Palma, the Virgen de las Nieves (Virgin of the Snows) is brought down from her hermitage on 5 August once every five years to the island capital of Santa Cruz. A month of lively celebrations ensues. The next descent is in the year 2005.

On El Hierro the Virgen de los Reyes (Virgin of the Kings) descends from her forest sanctuary to Valverde on the first weekend in July, once every four years. Her next journey is also in 2005.

Accommodation on both islands, scarce at the best of times, is much sought after during these periods.

Celebrations typically include a procession, either secular (marching bands and fancy costumes) or religious, depending upon the event. Sometimes it is a combination of both. The streets come alive with musicians, and food and drink vendors. Folk dancing, and sometimes Canarian wrestling (*see p159*) are staged. Fireworks often round off a fiesta, and revelries continue well into the small hours.

There are literally dozens of fiestas throughout the islands. Ask at the tourist office about local events during your stay. The most popular are listed below.

If you're not the sociable type or you value your sleep, then you may want to avoid certain places during *Carnaval*, and the

four- to five-yearly *Bajada* celebrations. Other fiestas are gentler, and should not disturb you unduly.

Carnaval (Carnival)
February
The big one (*see pp20–21*).

Semana Santa (Holy Week)
March–April
Hooded penitents progress through the streets.

Corpus Christi
June
This eight-day religious fiesta is the most important after *Carnaval*. The highlight is the 'flower carpets', made in many towns and villages. These are huge, colourful, pavement artworks (mostly floral or geometric, but sometimes in the form of

an Old Master), made of flower petals, coloured sand, or salt. La Orotava and La Laguna on Tenerife, and Las Palmas on Gran Canaria, are famous for their Corpus Christi carpets. These beautiful works of art are trampled underfoot by the devout during the procession.

If you are not on the islands during Corpus Christi, you may still be able to see a demonstration of 'sand-painting' at Casas de Los Balcones, La Orotava on Tenerife (*see p88*).

Romerías
June/July
A *romería* (pilgrimage) can be a most colourful celebration, particularly when the statue of the local Virgin is paraded through the streets on a highly decorated cart pulled by two dressed-up bullocks. There are two very good *romerías* on Tenerife: San Isidro at La Orotava in June, and San Benito Abad at La Laguna on the first Sunday in July.

Bajada de la Rama (Descent of the Branch)
4 August
This popular and joyful fiesta, held on 4 August at Agaete, Gran Canaria, is derived from an ancient Guanche rain-making ritual.

Canarians welcome any occasion to dress up and enjoy themselves

Carnaval

Carnaval (Carnival) is the biggest, costliest, most frenzied, and eagerly awaited event on the islands each year. As soon as one *Carnaval* is finished preparations begin for next year's extravaganza. It takes months to make some of the costumes, and the floats are often works of art. More than any other gesture, the huge sums of money spent on *Carnaval* by a people who are relatively poor, demonstrates their love of the fiesta.

Carnaval goes on for two hedonistic weeks with a programme of nightly outdoor dancing, usually to the hottest Latin American dance bands, fancy dress and drag competitions. Stalls selling *cubata* (rum and cola), *churros* (a type of Spanish doughnut), and *pinchitos* (kebabs) are everywhere.

Most of the big *Carnaval* attractions, called *cabalgatas*, take place at the weekend, so that people can lie in the day after celebrations. Many of the schools have their half-term at this time, so the smaller children can also have their fancy dress parties at school.

The highlight of all this activity is, of course, the main procession. Comparison with the famous Rio Carnival is obvious, and perhaps not surprising, given the number of Canarios who have emigrated to South America. Drummers beat out pulsating Latin rhythms, while the Carnival Queens stand proud on top of the procession floats in their magnificent dresses. The troupes alongside the floats, also in glitter, feathers, and often little else, rumba and samba along the procession route with the vitality and stamina of world-class athletes. Alongside them are drag queens, Charlie Chaplin and Fidel Castro look-alikes, plus a multitude of fancy-dressed children.

The *Murgas* are groups of men dressed alike in the costume theme of the year, who chant (rather like folklore rap) about various politicians or famous people and their 'gaffes'. In the past, when the government was more dictatorial, this was used as a form of satire against the various political institutions, without much risk of reprisal.

The most extraordinary sight during *Carnaval* is known as the Burial of the Sardine. An 8–10-m long cardboard/papier-mâché sardine is dragged to the harbour or the main square accompanied by mourners, invariably men dressed in black drag, theatrically 'weeping' and 'wailing' for all they are worth. At the appointed spot, fireworks inside the sardine are set off, and it literally blows itself apart. A grand firework display then follows.

The best places to catch *Carnaval* are Santa Cruz and Puerto de la Cruz on Tenerife, and Las Palmas, Gran Canaria. Dates vary. It starts first in Santa Cruz,

ending on Ash Wednesday, then fans out to all other points and other islands. Enquire at the tourist office in advance.

Colourful costumes compete for attention (and prizes) at the Puerto de la Cruz Carnival

Impressions

Over the last three decades, the Canary Islands have become as well known as the Spanish *costas* for a budget family playground of sun, sea, and sand. It is true that this type of holiday can be found in abundance in the southern resorts of Tenerife, Gran Canaria, and in certain parts of Lanzarote and Fuerteventura. But elsewhere on the islands there are few family tourism facilities, surprisingly little sand and, away from the southern shores, even the sun is not always reliable. All this means fewer people, which to some holidaymakers is an attraction in itself.

'The blue sky and all-pervading sun overhead, the delicious warmth but exquisite freshness of the air, all tell us that we have reached the haven of our rest. . .the Fortunate Islands.'

ERNEST HART

Letter to the *British Medical Journal* about Tenerife in 1887

Which Island?

If you're the social type and like to be among people of your own nationality, drinking in the types of bars you find at home and with all facilities laid on, then the southern resorts are for you. The highlights of all islands are well catered for by coach trips, so you don't even have to hire a car.

There's little to choose between Gran Canaria and Tenerife in terms of overall appeal. The former takes the lead in terms of beaches; the latter has more man-made attractions to enjoy. If you're still confused and think that the southern resorts of the big two islands sound over-commercialised, then Lanzarote may be the best choice. Fuerteventura is an island for beach-lovers and watersports fans. There's little else to see or do there.

At the other extreme, if you're the solitary type who takes pleasure in lonely walks, landscapes, and quiet local bars, one of the minor islands may well be your scene (though even among

these, El Hierro may be a little too quiet for most).

Of course, it's possible to get the best of both worlds – there is a handful of luxury hotels on La Gomera and La Palma which make 'going native' very painless. Or you could try self-catering on one of the larger islands. Good accommodation for the independent traveller, however, is not easy to find.

Island-hopping

There is no tradition of island-hopping in the Canaries, as there is on the Greek Islands. This is due to the distances involved, the packaged nature of Canarian holidays, which means few good budget hotels, and the packaged image of the islands, which in itself attracts a less adventurous type of traveller. Two-centre holidays are about as far as the genre goes. Tenerife/La Gomera and Lanzarote/Fuerteventura are the favourite combinations, due to their proximity and 35-minute sailing times, but it is possible to reach any of

the islands in under 45 minutes' flying time. Inter-island flights go via Gran Canaria for the eastern islands, and Tenerife (Los Rodeos, north airport) for the western islands.

All islands have their own airport. Fares are reasonable, check-in times are short, and it's an ideal way to sample the smaller islands for a day or two before committing yourself to a longer stay.

Rural and urban images: fieldworker on Tenerife (above); street sign on Gran Canaria (right)

Life on the smaller islands moves at a slow pace – goatherd on La Gomera

Cultural Differences

If you're familiar with mainland Spain then you won't find too much to surprise you in the Canary Islands. Tourism is so well established on all the islands, except El Hierro, that you'll very rarely have a problem making yourself understood, or finding what you want. However, this doesn't mean that you should assume everyone speaks English. A little Spanish will always be appreciated, and it's essential if you want to order something that is not on view, or ask what's cooking in the kitchen. In village bars they don't always have menus, or even food on display, but they'll usually be pleased to cook you a snack.

Don't forget the old tradition of the siesta. Villages and towns close down for the afternoon from around 1pm to 4 or 5pm. This isn't a good time to explore any settlement, as churches, museums, and shops will all be closed, and there will be a general ghost town atmosphere. It's much better to arrive in the early evening, when the Spanish tradition of the *paseo* (the promenade, or evening stroll) brings families out in their finery, and a lively atmosphere prevails in bars and cafés. When the *paseo* finishes, it is time to eat. The evening meal is generally taken around 8pm, a little later than in northern Europe, though early by Spanish mainland standards.

The beaches are a magnet for tourists and locals

WHAT'S IN A NAME

Surprising as it may seem, the Canary Islands are not named after the tiny yellow finch-like bird that inhabits the islands. In fact, it is the reverse, the birds taking their name from the islands (they also live on the other Macaronesian islands, *see p6*). If you want to glimpse a rare canary in the wild, look among stands of canary pines, though you'll have a much better chance of seeing them in cages outside village houses on Gran Canaria and Tenerife.

The most enduring legend associated with the name of the islands is that they were named after native dogs (*canes*, Spanish for canines) found by the early Mauretanian explorers. Today's *verdino*, the native Canarian dog, is presumed to be a descendant. If you don't see any real *verdinos*, look out for the famous statues by the cathedral in Las Palmas on Gran Canaria.

The black volcanic rocks of Playa de las Américas, Tenerife

Gran Canaria

Despite its name and fame, Gran Canaria isn't the biggest island of the Canaries (it is the third largest), yet somehow it feels big. In Las Palmas it has the most populous and dynamic city on the archipelago; Maspalomas is one of the largest resort complexes in Europe, and the inland scenery is grand in every sense. Only Tenerife can match its combination of cosmopolitan, rural, and seaside attractions, but there is no question that the beaches of Gran Canaria are far superior.

The island's comparatively small size can also be an advantage. Both Las Palmas and Maspalomas are just 30 minutes from the airport, and no place on the island is more than an hour's drive from either of these destinations. In fact, it's quite possible to drive round the whole island in a day, but it will be a very long day indeed!

Gran Canaria is the most popular island after Tenerife, but if you do wish to get away from it all you needn't worry about tourist hordes. The majority of visitors simply flop on to their towels and stay there, although an increasing number of tourists are now exploring and staying in the quieter rural areas.

Gran Canaria is often called 'a continent in miniature'; a reference to the extremes of landscape and climate that may be found on this island. Its landscapes change quickly from Wild West canyons to idyllic pine forests to Sahara-like dunes, and while there may be a dusting of snow on Pico de las Nieves, Maspalomas will still be wallowing in sun.

Gran Canaria is also culturally and historically the most well endowed of the islands. A rich collection of Guanche sites and relics is scattered around, and the best performing arts and museums are in Las Palmas.

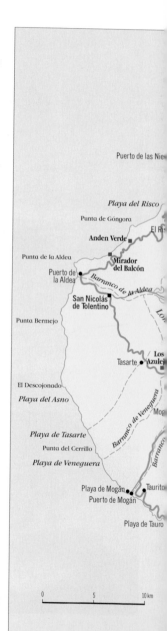

Gran Canaria

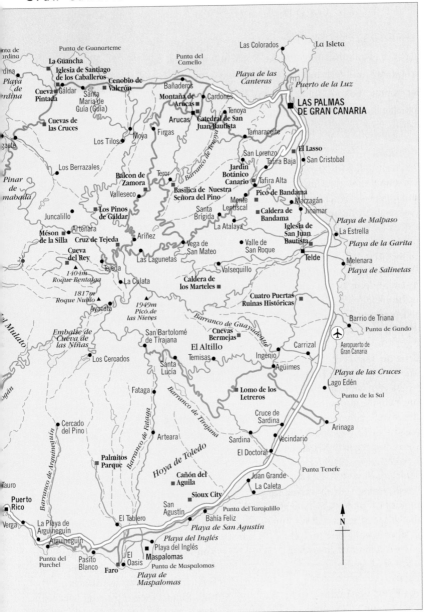

Punta de Guanarteme
Punta de Sardina
dina
Playa de Sardina
gaete

Las Colorados
La Isleta
Punta del Camello
Playa de las Canteras
Puerto de la Luz

La Guancha
Iglesia de Santiago de los Caballeros
Cenobio de Valerón
Bañaderos
Cueva Gáldar
Pintada
Santa María de Guía (Guía)
Montaña de Arucas
Cardones
Tenoya
LAS PALMAS DE GRAN CANARIA

Cuevas de las Cruces
Arucas
Catedral de San Juan Bautista
Firgas
Tamaraceite

Los Tilos
Moya

Los Berrazales

Pinar de mabada

San Lorenzo
El Lasso
Tafira Baja
San Cristobal

Balcón de Zamora
Teror
Jardín Botánico Canario
Tafira Alta

Vallseco
Basílica de Nuestra Señora del Pino
Monte Lentiscal
Pico de Bandama
Marzagán

Juncalillo
Los Pinos de Gáldar
Santa Brígida
La Atalaya
Caldera de Bandama
Jinámar

Playa de Malpaso
La Estrella

Mesón de la Silla
Artenara
Cruz de Tejeda
Aríñez
Vega de San Mateo
Valle de San Roque
Iglesia de San Juan Bautista
Playa de la Garita

Cueva del Rey
Las Lagunetas
Valsequillo
Telde
Melenara
Playa de Salinetas

1404m
Roque Bentaiga
Tejeda
La Culata
Caldera de los Marteles

1817m
Roque Nublo
1949m
Pico de las Nieves
Cuatro Puertas Ruinas Históricas

Ayacata

Barranco de Guayadeque
Barrio de Triana
Punta de Gando

Embalse de Cueva de las Niñas
San Bartolomé de Tirajana
Cuevas Bermejas
Carrizal
Aeropuerto de Gran Canaria

El Mulato
Los Cercados
El Altillo
Temisas
Ingenio
Agüimes

Santa Lucía
Playa de las Cruces
Lago Edén
Punta de la Sal

Fataga
Lomo de los Letreros

gán

Cercado del Pino
Arteara
Cruce de Sardina
Arinaga

Barranco de Arguineguín
Sardina
Vecindario

Palmitos Parque
Cañón del Águila
El Doctoral
Punta Tenefe

Tauro
Cañón del Águila
Juan Grande
La Caleta

Puerto Rico
Sioux City

Verga
San Agustín
Punta del Tarajalillo

La Playa de Arguineguín
El Tablero
Bahía Feliz
Playa de San Agustín

N

Arguineguín
Playa del Inglés
Playa del Inglés

Punta del Parchel
Pasito Blanco
El Oasis
Maspalomas
Faro
Punta de Maspalomas

Playa de Maspalomas

Barranco de Fataga

Hoya de Toledo

Barranco de Tirajana

Barranco de Tenoya

Central Gran Canaria

The heart of the island was once a sacred point for the Guanches, and their totem rocks, Nublo and Bentaiga, still dominate an epic mountain landscape. Breathtaking *miradores* (lookout points) are the hallmark of this area, peering down to all points of the island and beyond.

The Cross of Tejeda – a tourist attraction

Artenara

At an altitude of 1,200m, this peaceful whitewashed settlement, clinging to the mountainside, is certainly the highest, and arguably the most spectacular village on the island. The views across the ravine, either from the pretty terrace of the Méson de Silla restaurant, or from the square next to the church, are legendary. Not so well known, however, is the village's small cave-church (up the hill, opposite the main church).
18km northwest of Cruz de Tejeda.

Cruz de Tejeda

The Cruz de Tejeda is a busy crossroads where you will find all sorts of merchandise and refreshment, including the island's *parador* (*see p169*). Here, at an altitude of 1,490m, there are superb views of three major landmarks: Roque Bentaiga, Roque Nublo, and Mount Teide, on Tenerife. Don't miss the *cruz* (cross) itself – a finely carved stone cross in front of the *parador* terrace. Close by, the village of Tejeda enjoys a picturesque position among verdant hills.
43km southwest of Las Palmas, 45km north of Maspalomas.

Los Pinos de Gáldar

The *mirador* of 'the pines of Gáldar' is a vantage point unlike many in the mountainous interior. Here, the view stumbles over the edge of a crater, slides down verdant pine-covered hillsides, and descends for over 40km, taking in the whole of the north coast.
9km north of Cruz de Tejeda.

Pico de las Nieves

The 'Peak of the Snows' is the geographic centre and highest point of Gran Canaria at 1,949m above sea level. Cloud permitting, the views of the island's mountainous interior are quite stunning from here.
8km southeast of Cruz de Tejeda.

Pinar de Tamadaba

The *pinar* (pine forest) of Tamadaba is a beautiful area of tall, slender pines to the northwest of Artenara. A narrow circular road snakes up to around 1,400m and, if the weather is clear, rewards you with a priceless view of Mount Teide, floating above the clouds.
25km northwest of Cruz de Tejeda.

Roque Bentaiga/Cueva del Rey

Roque Bentaiga was a sacred spot to the Guanches, and goats were once sacrificed on the simple altar which still stands here. It's possible to walk up to the summit (1,404m), but you must be very sure-footed and have a head for heights. Along the same track (past the Bentaiga turning) is the **Cueva del Rey** (King's Cave). Stop your car when a tall crag looms to your left, and the road dives downhill to your right. Walk round the mountainside to your left, and the Cueva del Rey, once the royal abode, is high above in the honeycombed rock. The views from here, across to Artenara, are truly fit for a king. It is possible to climb right up to the caves, but be very careful if you do.

As if to confirm the Guanches' mystic views, from certain angles, the rock next to Bentaiga takes on the appearance of a robed holy man – hence its name, Roque El Fraile ('The Monk').
On the C811 between Cruz de Tejeda and Ayacata (44km from Las Palmas).

Roque Nublo (Cloud Rock)
It is claimed that this landmark pinnacle, pointing 1,803m into the Canarian sky, is the world's highest basalt monolith. Like Roque Bentaiga, this, too, was once a holy site. If you want to walk to the rock, it's just over 6km from the nearest accessible approach point of La Culata.
La Culata is 1km north of Ayacata.

Enhanced by the early light of dawn, Roque Bentaiga provides a primordial landscape

The flower-filled valley of
Barranco de Guaydeque

Eastern Gran Canaria

It may be hard to believe that there is life beyond the
soulless strip of the GC1 motorway and barren east coast,
but just a few kilometres inland are wealthy villages, a sub-
tropical *barranco* (ravine), a colonised crater, and the
island's second city.

Bandama (Caldera de/Pico de)
The volcano of Bandama rises to 569m
and is a popular *mirador*, looking into
the crater (*see pp50–51*) and across to
Las Palmas. The Golf Club de
Bandama enjoys a magnificent setting.
10km south of Las Palmas.

Barranco de Guayadeque
The lush and spectacular ravine of
Guayadeque drains almost from the
centre of the island to the coast. From
the visitor's viewpoint, however, it starts
gradually at Agüimes, with banana
plantations giving way to tall palms and
wild cacti as the valley sides rise. After
5km, the **Cuevas Bermejas** (Purple
Caves) are the first sign that this was
once a Guanche stronghold. Here, latter-
day troglodytes have their homes, keep
animals, and have built a cave chapel.

Soon, the valley sides rise to 300m
high, and in spring the area is a riot of
pink almond blossom. After another
3km the road ends at the Montaña de
las Tierras, where there are more caves
(old and new) and refreshments.
*Just outside Agüimes (14km south of
Telde). On the road in from the GC1 look
for a small sign on the right-hand side
before Agüimes centre which leads to the
Cruce Arinaga/Crocodile Park, whose*

*resident reptiles enthral children.
Tel: (928) 784725.
www.cocodrilopark.vrcanaries.com*

Cuatro Puertas
This has one of the most interesting
aboriginal sites on the island, the Holy
Mountain of the Guanches, dating from
the palaeolithic period.
*Situated between Ingenio and Telde on
the C815.*

Ingenio
Ingenio is a prosperous market town
that also boasts a tradition of
handicrafts. You can visit some of the
town's *artesanías* (craft workshops) on
the main road towards Telde (the C816
road). Also on this road, just outside
town, is the **Museo de Piedras y
Artesanía Canaria** (Museum of Rocks
and Canarian handicrafts). It's a strange
mix of old-fashioned geological exhibits,
bygones, embroidery, and gaudy
religious displays.
*Ingenio is 12km south of Telde. Museum
open: daily 9am–6pm. Free admission.*

Jardín (Botánico) Canario
Founded in 1952 on a steep hillside, this
is the island's most comprehensive
garden. It has as near natural conditions

as possible. Virtually every type of plant indigenous to the island grouping of Macaronesia can be seen here (*see pp92–3*).

La Calzada, near Tafira Alta, 7km southwest of Las Palmas. Open: daily (except 1 Jan & Good Friday) 9am–6pm. Free admission.
Tel: (928) 219582/354613.

Tafira/Santa Brígida/Vega de San Mateo

This triumvirate of villages, already prosperous from the rich farming communities around them, has been colonised by the well-to-do of Las Palmas. Vega de San Mateo is the most interesting of the three, with a busy Sunday livestock market, and the ethnological museum of **Casa de Cho Zacharías**, with a collection of agricultural equipment and craft work. Aside from this there is little formal sightseeing, but the area provides a pleasant drive out from Las Palmas, past handsome villas, expensive restaurants, and views down into verdant valleys.

Southwest of Las Palmas, Tafira 8km, Santa Brígida 15km, Vega de San Mateo 20km. Museum: Tel: (928) 640627. Open: Mon–Sat 9am–1pm (telephone to arrange tour with guide). Closed: Sun.

Telde

Gran Canaria's second city owes its wealth to its 16th-century sugarcane trade, and grand mansions of this period can be found in the San Juan district to the north of the town. In the same quarter is the jewel of the city – the richly decorated 15th-century Iglesia de San Juan de Bautista (Church of St John the Baptist). It has a splendidly carved early 16th-century Flemish altarpiece and, from the same period, an intriguing life-size figure of Christ, made in Mexico from corn husks and weighing just 5kg.

The centre of Telde is now a one-way street system with many interesting small shops, and a market on Saturday mornings.

14km south of Las Palmas. The Church of St John the Baptist is in the Plaza de San Juan Bautista. Open: for services only.

Vecindario

This typically Spanish town is gradually transforming itself into a place for tourists to visit. It has a large new commercial centre, an airport, hotel, and a cinema that shows up-to-date films in English some afternoons. Most people find a Wednesday morning browsing around the market, followed by lunch in one of the many cafés or restaurants, and then a walk around the commercial centre, a good day out.

15km north of Playa del Inglés on the C812. There is a good bus service.

Telde's wealth of Spanish colonial buildings is the legacy of 16th-century sugarcane traders

Las Palmas

Las Palmas, the biggest city on the archipelago (population 366,000) is a major port, an historic capital, a business centre, and a holiday resort. Not so long ago it was *the* fashionable Canarian resort, but nowadays most holidaymakers head to the purpose-built southern developments, where sunshine is virtually guaranteed, and a 'real British pub' is never far away.

The golden crescent of Canteras Beach

Las Palmas is not to everyone's taste. It's busy, noisy, run-down in parts, and suffers from petty crime and traffic problems. But there is more Spanish atmosphere, history, and culture to enjoy here than anywhere else on the island.
Las Palmas is 58km north of Maspalomas. Tourist Office: Parque de Santa Catalina. Tel: (928) 264623. Open: Mon–Fri 9am–1.30pm & 5–7pm, Sat 9.30am–1pm.

Alfredo Kraus Auditorium and Parliament Building

The work of architect Oscar Turquets, this comprises eleven sound-proofed chambers, seven of them bearing the names of the various Canary Islands, and the Symphony Hall, which has an enormous window behind the stage overlooking the sea. The Gran Canarian Philharmonic Orchestra is based here.
For information and tickets: Tel: (902) 405504/115188/(928)247442; fax: (928) 276042. www.festivaldecanarias.com

Casa de Colón (House of Columbus)

The House of Columbus belonged to the island's first governor, and dates originally from the 15th century. Columbus stayed here on two or three

occasions en route to the New World. A museum with exhibits relating to his journeys, and a Museum of Fine Art are housed in the building.
Calle de Colón 1, Vegueta. Tel: (928) 312373/311255. Open: Mon–Fri 9am–7pm, Sat & Sun 9am–3pm. Free admission. Guided tours on request.

Catedral de Santa Ana (Cathedral of St Ana)

From the outside there is little to commend this huge, grimy building. Construction began in 1497, but it was still being built in the 20th century. Inside, however, there are many treasures. Its **Museo Diocesano de Arte Sacro** (Diocesan Museum of Sacred Art) boasts a rich collection of statues, paintings, and gold and silver ware.

The Plaza de Santa Ana in front of the cathedral is a handsome square with the *ayuntamiento* (town hall) at the far end, and to the right, the **Palacio Episcopal** (Bishop's Palace).
Plaza de Santa Ana. Tel: (928) 313600. Museum open: during service hours. Admission charge.

Las Palmas de Gran Canaria

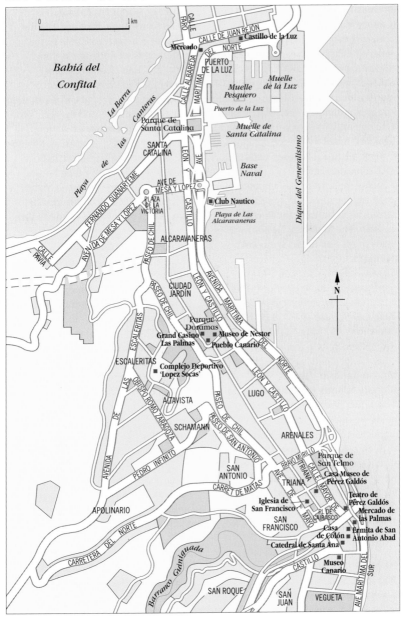

Dormas Parque/Pueblo Canario (Canary Village)

The centrepiece of this pleasant, grassy park is the Pueblo Canario, an idealised re-creation of a typical village, including a church, a *bodega* (wine bar), shops, a tourist office, and the Museo de Néstor, arranged around a pretty square. Come here on Sunday between 11.30am and 1pm, or Thursday between 5.30pm and 7.00pm, when a folk group entertains with song and dance.

Néstor de la Torre was a famous local artist and designer who conceived, among other projects, the Pueblo Canario. The Museo de Néstor features many of his best exotic Symbolist paintings.

Pueblo Canario. Tel: (928) 245135. Open: Tue–Fri 10am–1pm & 4–8pm, Sun 11am–2pm. Admission charge. Tourist Office: Tel: (928) 243593/362222. Open: Mon–Fri 9am–1.30pm & 5–7pm, Sat 9.30am–1pm.

Museo Canario (Canary Islands Museum)

This rather old-fashioned museum holds the finest collection of Guanche artefacts in the whole archipelago. Along with everyday grave finds, there is a startling display of skulls and mummies which will delight older children.

Calle Dr Chil 25. Tel: (928) 336800. Open: Mon–Fri 10am–8pm, Sat 10am–2pm, Sun 10am–2pm. Admission charge.

Playa de las Canteras

This long, golden, crescent-shaped beach is one of the longest city beaches in the world, extending for 2.6km on the northwest side of Las Palmas. It is conveniently protected from Atlantic rollers by a natural reef close to the shore, and is ideal for safe bathing. There are clean changing rooms, showers and toilets for a small fee. Those in search of wind and waves need only venture out beyond the reef. The promenade is lined with restaurants of many nationalities – Bulgarian, Korean, and Japanese sit alongside British, German, and Swedish eating houses, reflecting the home countries of the sailors who take 'rest and recreation' here alongside ordinary holidaymakers.

Puerto de la Luz

Las Palmas was once one of the busiest ports in the western hemisphere. Today, it still throbs with activity with up to 1,000 ships a month passing through, but it has lost much of its vitality. The number of sailors has diminished as cargo-handling has become less labour-intensive, and few ocean liners now call here.

The port is at its most colourful on Sunday mornings, when the *rastro* (flea-market) on the Avenida Marítima is patronised by locals, tourists, and a good number of West African shoppers and vendors. Nearby, in Calle de Juan Rejón, the sturdy stone **Castillo de la Luz** (castle), built in 1494, is the oldest building on Gran Canaria. It is occasionally open for special exhibitions.

Santa Catalina

This is the bustling area behind the beach, jam-packed with duty-free shops, hotels, restaurants, bars, and the red-light district. The hub of the area is the

cosmopolitan pedestrianised garden square of Parque de Santa Catalina. Here you will find Europeans, Africans, and North Americans enjoying a drink, and indulging in the park's favourite pastime of people-watching. There are also many leisure attractions, such as a children's play area, a board-games area, and so on, and on Sunday lunchtimes a musical band entertains the public.
Tourist Office: Tel: (928) 264623.

Triana

Triana is the city's original commercial district. The area's main thoroughfare is the pedestrianised shopping street of Calle Mayor de Triana. At its northern end is the charming **Parque de San Telmo**, with a chapel and some fine dragon trees. Towards the southern end of the street at No. 6 Calle Cano lies the **Casa Museo de Pérez Galdós**, former home of one of the island's favourite writers, born here in 1843. The handsome 1919 Teatro de Pérez Galdós opera house is close by.

Just off the north end of Calle Mayor are the beautiful squares of San Francisco and Cairasco. The former houses a fine bust of Columbus, and the lovely 17th-century

Iglesia de San Francisco. The Plaza de Cairasco is notable for the 100-year-old **Gabinete Literario** (Literary Cabinet Institute), elegantly arcaded and stuccoed, and occasionally open to the public for exhibitions (enquire at the tourist information office).
Casa Museo de Pérez Galdós, Calle Cano 6. Tel: (928) 366976. Open: Mon–Fri 9am–8pm, Sat 9am–3pm.
Closed: weekends. Free admission.

Vegueta Quarter

This is the oldest part of town, where the Castilian conquerors landed in 1478. It became the district where the ruling classes lived, and it still retains an aristocratic air, with splendid 17th- and 18th-century mansions decorated with coats of arms and elegantly crafted balconies. The shady squares and worn cobbled streets have changed little since Columbus's day, and you can visit the Casa de Colón, where he stayed (*see p32*) and see the Ermita (Church) de San Antonio Abad, where he prayed. The latter was rebuilt in the 18th century, but is rarely open to the public. Vegueta is also home to the Catedral de Santa Ana (*see p32*).

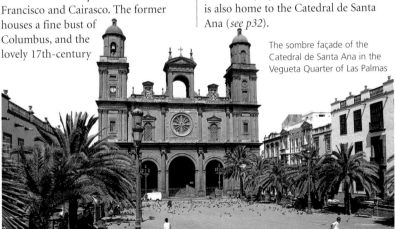

The sombre façade of the Catedral de Santa Ana in the Vegueta Quarter of Las Palmas

Christopher Columbus

Christopher Columbus (Cristóbal Colón in Spanish) used the Canary Islands on several occasions as a staging post for his voyages to the New World. The records of his visits vary, and different sources argue about where he was on any one occasion. There is agreement, however, that he did stop off at Las Palmas and La Gomera in 1492.

On Gran Canaria, Columbus may have dropped anchor at Gando Bay (where the airport now is), or near the site of the present-day Puerto de la Luz in Las Palmas. From his own diary we know that just as he was passing Tenerife, Mount Teide erupted, and this was taken as an ill omen by his superstitious crew.

Columbus also stopped at La Gomera to take on water and other supplies, but another reason he may have wanted to stop here was to see the Countess of Gomera, Beatriz de Bobadilla (see p113). Columbus probaby knew her from the Spanish Court – he was sailing under the flag of Ferdinand and Isabella – and there are rumours of an affair.

Columbus may have returned to La Gomera on his voyages of 1493–5 and 1498–1500. It is also thought that he visited Las Palmas on at least two occasions (either during the afore-mentioned dates, or on his last voyage of 1502–4). Other records mention Maspalomas on Gran Canaria and El Hierro as stopping points.

Local latter-day reactions to the great explorer are mixed. While Gran Canarios don't seem unduly disturbed by modern inter-pretations of Columbus as hero or villain (Colón is, after all, derived from the Spanish word for 'colonialism'), Gomerans take a sterner view. They no doubt remember that Columbus was involved with the slave trade, and was, at the very least, friendly with the Countess Beatriz, who tyrannised the island. Graffiti against the celebrations which marked the 500th anniversary of the 'Discovery' were widely seen in the island capital in 1992. The resistance to the Spanish Conquest was as fierce on La Gomera as anywhere. It seems that memories here are also very long.

COLÓN

Above: Columbus's house in Las Palmas. Facing page: statue in the Fundación César Manrique

Maspalomas

As surely as nature has created the rugged interior of Gran
Canaria, so developers have created the streamlined
holiday world of Maspalomas – the 'Costa Canaria'. It will
either distress or reassure you to learn that this is one of the
three biggest resort complexes under the Spanish flag, on
the same scale as Benidorm and Torremolinos. First
impressions are inauspicious, as serried ranks of high-rise
towers loom next to the motorway. Beyond this, however,
most of the developments are nearer the ground, and the
beaches are the finest on the island.

Fataga village near
Maspalomas

Dunas de Maspalomas
(Dunes of Maspalomas)

Spectacular desert-like dunes are the
trademark of this area. Despite their
Saharan appearance they were not
blown in from Africa (as was once
thought), nor were they shipped here as
a tourist attraction (as was Las Teresitas
beach on Tenerife). They are a product
of sea and wind forces peculiar to this
area. The dunes have always been
protected from development, but
anybody is free to walk across them.
Don't be surprised if you are confronted
by nudists or a tourist camel train; both
use the dunes frequently. One of the
best views of the dunes is at sunset from
the terrace of the Hotel Riu Palace in
Playa del Inglés.

Maspalomas (Faro)

Rather confusingly, the name
Maspalomas refers not only to the larger
Costa Canaria conurbation, but also to
the original oasis area of Maspalomas,
which includes Playa del Inglés and San

Agustín. Until the early 1960s this was
simply an oasis by the dunes, with a
freshwater pool, a palm grove, and a
lighthouse (*faro*) which dates from 1886.
All of this remains, but nowadays the
oasis is the preserve of luxury hotels.
The 6-km long beach has an exotic
backdrop, more intimate than the long,
featureless stretches just to the east.
Aside from the hotels and resorts, a
promenade is being built from here to
Pasito Blanco. The rest of Maspalomas –
largely self-catering bungalows – clusters
around a championship golf course,
before merging almost imperceptibly
into Playa del Inglés.

The resort's biggest man-made
attraction is **Holiday World**, the first
amusement park in the Canaries. All the
usual favourites are here: a landmark
ferris wheel, swingboats, bumping cars
(and boats), phantom jets, and so on.
*Maspalomas Faro is 58km south of Las
Palmas. For tourist information see Playa
del Inglés. Holiday World is open: daily
6pm–midnight. Tel: (928) 762982;*

fax: (928)766355; brusty@arrakis.es
Admission charge (covers all rides).

Pasito Blanco

This new marina development with
berthing room for up to 500 pleasure
craft occupies a pretty cove. Big-game
fishing boats can be hired, and it's
always interesting to see the catches
being proudly exhibited late in the
afternoon.
6km west of Maspalomas Faro.

Playa del Inglés

The name of this resort, 'Beach of the
English', is somewhat misleading; you
will find many different north European
nationalities here. It was created on
barren land during the 1960s, and has
become a super-compressed labyrinth of
hotels, apartments, cheap restaurants,
bars, and ugly *Centros Commerciales*
(shopping centres). The only points of
sightseeing interest are the intriguing
Ecumenical Church, which resembles a
portion of the Sydney Opera House, and
the **Insular Tourism Centre**, which
doubles as a tourist information and
cultural centre. Here handicrafts are on
sale, and local musicians give concerts.
*5km east of Maspalomas Faro. Insular
Tourism Centre: Avenida España/Estados
Unidos. Tel: (928) 771550. Open: Mon–
Fri 9am–9pm; shops 9am–1pm & 4–7pm.*

Natural forces have bestowed Maspalomas with this spectacular dunescape

The Ecumenical Church at Playa del Inglés

San Fernando

This residential area lies behind Playa del Inglés. It has a newly built shopping centre with an excellent supermarket called the Bella Vista, well worth visiting for self-catering tourists who like a larger selection of groceries for their day-to-day meals.

San Agustín

Although the very first hotel on the Costa Canaria sprang up here in the

early 1960s, San Agustín has remained the most restrained of the three resorts, largely given over to low-rise apartments with attractive gardens. It draws an older clientele who don't seem to mind that their beach is the darkest coloured of the three, although it does have the advantage of a low cliff backing.
9km east of Maspalomas Faro.

Sioux City

This 'paella-Western' theme park occupies a canyon with genuine Wild West scenery.

Stunt men act out bank hold-ups, shoot-outs, and lynchings, Mexican hombres perform knife-throwing acts, and a routine from the saloon gals and boys reduces the adrenaline before a cowboy barbecue.

3km north of San Agustín. Cañon del Aguila. Tel: (928) 762573. Open: Tue–Sun 10am–late evening. Shows (knife-throwing, shooting, and lassoing, etc). Western night barbecue dinner on Fri 8pm. Admission charge. Bus: No. 29.

MASPALOMAS ENVIRONS
Fataga

This charming oasis settlement lies in the middle of the 'Valley of a Thousand Palms'. A handful of whitewashed houses and shops, a small archetypal church, a bar, and a restaurant comprise the prettiest small village on the island. The adjacent palm-filled Barranco de Fataga is popular for its camel farms and camel safaris.
20km north of Maspalomas Faro.

White-washed stone walls, red-tiled roofs, and exotic plants result in a charming rural picture

Mundo Aborigen (Aboriginal World)

Situated in the mountains looking down on to Playa del Inglés/Maspalomas, this interesting historical theme park deals with the living habits of Guanches and re-creates the way they lived.

6km on the road from Playa del Inglés to Fataga. Tel: (928) 172295. Open: Mon–Fri 8.30–11am & 3–6.30pm, Sun & holidays 8am–3pm. Bus: No. 18.

Palmitos Parque

Set in beautifully landscaped gardens in a dramatic canyon, this is the finest bird park on the islands. The caged birds are well displayed, with abundant greenery softening the feeling of captivity. What makes this park special, however, is the number of free-flying species. It's exhilarating to see toucans and other brightly coloured birds flying and nesting in the palms above. There's also a parrot show and one of the biggest butterfly houses in Europe, with hundreds of exquisite tropical varieties flying freely.

10km north of Maspalomas Faro. Tel: (928) 140276. Open: daily 9am–6pm. Admission charge. Bus: No. 45.

San Bartolomé de Tirajana

The rustic streets and earthy bars of this small agricultural village are a perfect antidote to the contrived resort life of the coast. The best time to visit is on a Sunday morning, when a lively market springs up. The present village church dates from 1903, and contains a statue of St James (Santiago) which was held in the 15th-century hermitage on the same site. It shows Santiago in his traditional Spanish role as 'Moor-slayer'. The statue

The lush, fertile oasis town of Fataga is situated in a barren mountainous landscape

Palmitos Parque is a showcase for native flora and fauna

was brought here during the Conquest in the hope that it would have the same evangelising effect on the Guanches.

Walk up the hill and you will find many old houses. The House of Tunte (the Guanche name for the village) and the Corner of Tunte in Princesa Guayarmina alleyway both date from the 15th century.

28km north of Maspalomas Faro.

Santa Lucía de Tirajana

From San Bartolomé the road snakes down to the east, through a fertile valley to the pretty village of Santa Lucía. The church here is a landmark for miles around, with a large, white Moorish dome. In front are luxurious, well-

tended gardens. A little way past the village is the private **Museo Castillo de la Fortaleza**. The castle in question is a new, small mock-fortress with dusty displays on archaeology, fossils, and ethnography (including a 16th-century bedroom), among other exhibits. Don't miss the fine display of paintings upstairs. The museum boasts a lovely garden, complete with rusting cannons, and a charming outdoor restaurant.

Santa Lucía is 31km north of Maspalomas Faro. Church open: Mon–Sat 10am–5pm, Sun noon–4pm. Admission charge. The museum is on the C815 road, 1km north of the village. Tel: (928) 798310. Open: daily 10am–6.30pm. Admission charge.

Northern Gran Canaria

If you are in search of typical Gran Canarian settlements, head north. The small towns and villages here are self-contained farming communities and rely neither on tourism nor on the wealth of Las Palmas. The coast road provides spectacular views down to the wild northwest fringes and across to Tenerife.

'God's Finger' at Puerto de las Nieves

Agaete

This picturesque small town lies in a particularly fertile belt, with coffee and exotic fruits among its many crops. Its showpiece is the **Huerto de las Flores** (Garden of the Flowers), a garden of tropical and subtropical plants. In the town square old men doze on park benches in front of the large, red-domed church. La Virgen de las Nieves is well worth a visit, as is the nearby archaeological excavation site of Malpais.

The port of Agaete, Puerto de las Nieves, where the Fred Olsen ferry to Tenerife is based, is a windswept spot with a small promenade overlooking wild cliff scenery and a black pebble beach. The famous rock, **Dedo de Dios** (Finger of God), is seen here.
41km west of Las Palmas. Huerto de las Flores is a small enclosed park in the centre of the village. Open: dawn to dusk. Free admission.

Arucas

A towering, Neo-Gothic cathedral is the last thing you would expect to see in the midst of a whitewashed Canarian farming community. It was started in 1909 and completed in the late 1970s as an ostentatious sign of the town's wealth – founded in no small part on the locally produced rum (*ron*), on sale on all the islands. Near the church is a small botanic garden (the Parque Municipal) and a statue to the Guanche king, Doramas. Legend has it that he was slain treacherously while challenging the *conquistador* Pedro de Vera to single combat on Montaña de Arucas in 1481.
17km west of Las Palmas.

Gáldar

This busy, workaday town, once the capital of the island, has several points of interest. In the main square, look inside the courtyard of the Town Hall (open weekday mornings only), where the ancient dragon tree is said to be the oldest on the island. Ask here about visits to the Cueva Pintada. Also in the square is the Iglesia de Santiago de los Caballeros, a church dating from 1872 and containing many fine sculptures.

The **Cueva Pintada** (Painted Cave), at the southwest end of town, is a small Guanche cave with painted geometric figures, only discovered in 1873. It has, however, been closed for many years while undergoing restoration work. The other Guanche legacy nearby (in a neglected state) is an 11th-century

cemetery, thought to be the last resting place of Guanche nobles.
31km west of Las Palmas.

Reptilandia
This zoological park in Gáldar contains more than 500 species from scorpions, tarantulas, turtles to lizards, crocodiles, iguanas, and also monkeys.
Snake and other reptile feeding is on Sun at 3pm. Tel: (928) 551269; Fax: (928) 551242. Open: daily 11am–5.30pm, except Christmas & New Year's Day.

(Santa Maria de) Guía
In the centre of Guía is a pretty square with an imposing Neo-Classical church and narrow streets running off it. The main attraction, however, is the **Cenobio de Valerón** (Convent of Valeron) to the east of town. This is a honeycomb of Guanche caves set in a sheer rock face, to which new concrete steps (190 in all) offer access. Despite fanciful legends that these were once priestesses' and virgins' lodgings, the caves were probably just a grain store.
28km west of Las Palmas. Caves open: Tue–Sun 10am–1pm & 3–5pm. Free admission.

Teror
Architecturally, this is the most typical Canarian town on the island, with beautifully preserved white houses and dozens of perfectly carved wooden balconies. It is also the religious centre of Gran Canaria, with a statue of the Virgin housed in the town's splendid 18th-century basilica. The only house open to the public is the atmospheric 17th-century **Casa de los Patronos de la Virgen del Pino**, now a museum with a beautiful patio. Shops sell traditional lace and scents made from local flora.
23km southwest of Las Palmas. Museum tel: (928) 630239. Open: 10am–5pm. Admission charge.

The church of Arucas dominates the countryside

Western Gran Canaria

Until quite recently the west of Gran Canaria was little visited, and even today the coast north of Puerto de Mogán is undeveloped. The southwest corner, however, is a conservationist's nightmare, with row upon row of white boxes obscuring the hillsides. The development of Puerto de Mogán itself partly redresses these excesses, while the natural scenery beyond it is spectacular.

Arguineguín

Arguineguín, not to be confused with the adjacent La Playa de Arguineguín/Patalavaca tourist development, is the only genuine fishing village on this part of the coast. Market day, Tuesday, is the best time to visit; there is also a daily fish auction at the port.
12km west of Maspalomas.

Cactualdea

These gardens lie just north of San Nicolas de Tolentino, and have a wonderful collection of plants and cacti from the archipelago.
Tel: (928) 891228.

Mogán

This small, pretty, quiet hill village is a breath of fresh air after the overcrowded coastal strip – its gardens and countryside abound with exotic tropical fruits and flowers. For a picnic,

take the minor C811 road 10km north to the beautifully situated **Embalse de Cueva de las Niñas** ('The Little Girls' Cave Reservoir') which has barbecue facilities.

Another point of outstanding natural beauty, **Los Azulejos**, lies 11km north of Mogán on the road to San Nicolás.
Mogán is 9km north of Puerto de Mogán.

Playa de Amodores

This is a beautiful, new, man-made beach within a sheltered bay with shower and toilet facilities. There are cafés and restaurants nearby. You need to get there by bus or car.
5km west of Puerto Rico.

Puerto de Mogán

Puerto de Mogán is a good example of sympathetic Canarian holiday development. The old

PUTTING TO SEA

Most holidaymakers on this coast will be tempted on to at least one sea excursion. Options include a lazy day on the fully rigged *Windjammer San Miguel*, a shark-fishing adventure or a *Yellow Submarine* voyage. The latter is certainly the most novel ride, but it is expensive, and aside from a couple of wrecks, there is little to see.

The *Lineas Salmon* boat provides a useful regular transport service between Arguineguín, Puerto Rico, and Puerto de Mogán.

Lineas Salmon
Tel: (928) 243708.

Windjammer San Miguel
Tel: (928) 760076.
Departs daily from Puerto Rico at 10.30am.

Yellow Submarine
Tel: (928) 565108;
Fax: (928) 565048.
Departs from Puerto de Mogán harbour.

fishing harbour has been expanded to a traffic-free 'village' of local-style houses, painted white with a pastel trim, each with a wrought-iron balcony and pretty window boxes or garden. The houses cluster around a new pleasure marina, joined coherently by arches and bridges. Shops and restaurants are well-kept.

The original fishing fleet is still here and gives a genuine local touch to the marina. There is a small black beach next to the port, but most visitors prefer to make the short boat trip to the golden sands of Puerto Rico.
32km west of Maspalomas.

Puerto Rico

With its wonderful location in a crescent-shaped bay and stretches of golden sand, it's no wonder that Puerto Rico is popular. However, like many popular resorts it can get overcrowded.

The other appeal of Puerto Rico lies in its watersports and fishing facilities. It has the best pleasure harbour on the island, and both its sailing school and its fishing charters enjoy international fame.
18km west of Maspalomas.

San Nicolás de Tolentino

San Nicolás is a major agricultural centre in a fertile valley. Its great silvery netted greenhouse-like fields are landmarks which can be seen as far away as the centre of the island. The straggling town itself is of no great interest, but its port (known as Puerto de la Aldea) is worth a visit for its fish restaurants and the views from its attractive black pebble beach. San Nicolás is also the gateway to the island's most spectacular drive (*see p48*).
64km northwest of Maspalomas.

The new marina complex at Puerto de Mogán – all neat and tidy and shipshape

Drive: Route of the Reservoirs

This excursion through the wild interior of the island is as spectacular a route as any on the archipelago, climbing from an altitude of 64m to 1,200m. This is a favourite route for organised jeep safaris, but although the road is rough in parts, a four-wheel drive vehicle is not necessary. However, the narrow, winding roads are often unprotected from steep drops, so care and confidence are needed. Don't attempt it in an ordinary car if the weather is poor. The route is just 29km long, but driving conditions are slow. *Allow 2 hours.*

Start from the centre of San Nicolás de Tolentino. Follow the small yellow directional arrow to Artenara (left, right, and left again).

The Parralillo reservoir with Roque Bentaiga in the background

1 San Nicolás

The route starts on narrow tracks set amid tall fields of tomatoes and papayas and ramshackle smallholdings.

Leaving the fields, the road climbs sharply, following the line of the Barranco de la Aldea, and is very rough. After around 7km, it flattens out and becomes smoother. There is a bar and the Embalse (Reservoir) del Caidero to your right.

By now the scenery is breathtaking, with peak upon peak rising sharply as far as the eye can see. The valley floor is lush around the reservoirs, but the mountains are stark in greys, and shades of red and pink.

A little further on to the right the clear blue waters of the Presa de Siberio come into view (a *presa* is a small reservoir).

The road climbs up to a mirador (16km past San Nicolás), where the shell of a small windmill, minus its sails, now resembles a sentry box. From here

there are wonderful views down to the Embalse de Parralillo and the Presa de Siberio.

2 Embalse de Parralillo (Parralillo Reservoir)

This is the most striking of all the reservoirs. If the light is right it will take on a deep, emerald green hue, but in any shade of blue or green it is a fine sight. Across to the east you can see quite clearly the Guanches' sacred rocks of Bentaiga (large and square), and behind it, to the right, Nublo, a smaller, though higher pinnacle (*see p29*).

The road climbs slowly up towards the centre of the island, approaching Roque Bentaiga. After 22km the route reaches the village of Acusa.

3 Acusa

The Route of the Reservoirs ends in green fields near Acusa, at the Church of La Candelaria.

Way down below, to the left, is the last of the reservoirs, the Presa de la Candelaria. (If you would like to see some cave dwellings, follow the sign to Acusa.)

Unless you are visiting the caves, keep on the road left to Artenara. Turn right at the Cruz de Acusa crossroads at 26km, and after a further 3km you will come to Artenara (see p28).

4 Artenara

To end the trip on a high note, enjoy the magnificent views from the church square or make your way for a typically Canarian snack to the Méson de la Silla restaurant (on the road directly above the approach road to the village), where the view is just as spectacular, and even more beautifully framed.

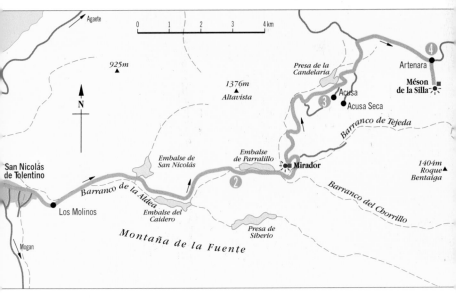

Walk: Caldera de Bandama

The Caldera de Bandama is said to be the most perfectly formed volcanic crater in the Canary Islands. Each year, thousands of coach trippers gaze down into the *caldera* from the *mirador* (lookout point) above – yet very few tourists (or even locals) actually venture down to the valley floor. It's a short but very steep trek to this tiny Shangri-la. Anyone who is moderately fit can do the walk. If it's a nice day, take a drink and picnic.
Allow 1½ hours.

GRAN CANARIA

Las P
de G
Cana

Caldera de
Bandama ■

San Nicolás
de Tolentino

▲
Pico de
las Nieves

■ Maspalomas

The unique environment of the Caldera fosters a distinctive ecology

FRAGILE WORLD

The Caldera de Bandama is of great interest. Guanche caves are located on the sheer, higher levels, though only the more daring try to explore them. Botanists also come down into the valley to conduct plant trials in this unique environment. Unfortunately, tourist coaches are causing the side of the crater to slip away (there are plans to re-route heavy vehicles). Walkers should also be sensitive to the environment, and stay on the given paths in order to prevent damage to plant-life and the environment.

Follow the roadsigns for the Campo de Golf, and park as close to the Hotel de Golf as possible.

The views to either side of the road are magnificent. To the *caldera* side you can see the whole of the 1,000m-diameter crater opening before you; to the golf club side you can see far beyond the club house and hotel, with carpets of green leading to the distant hills.

Walk back along the road for half a kilometre until you come to the Restaurant Los Geranios. Go down the short road between the restaurant and bus stop and you will come to the steps leading down into the caldera.

After 20 or so large steps the path becomes a narrow dirt track. Don't worry about getting lost – there's just one way, and that's down, 200m to the

valley floor. It only takes 15 minutes to make the steep descent but it will take you much longer to get back up.

Towards the bottom of the track you will see, down to the left, the farm where an elderly farmer still lives and works. This path is his only contact with the outside world.

Once on the valley floor, follow the path leading between the drystone walls to the tall, shady eucalyptus trees. In winter, the valley floor is a splendid sight, carpeted with bright yellow flowering trefoils, divided neatly by drystone walls and decorated by tall palms and fruit-laden orange trees. The whole scene, complete with its low rustic farmhouses and grazing goats, is more akin to a rather exotic English meadow than an arid Canarian island.

This is effectively the centre of the caldera. *Retrace your route to the starting point.*

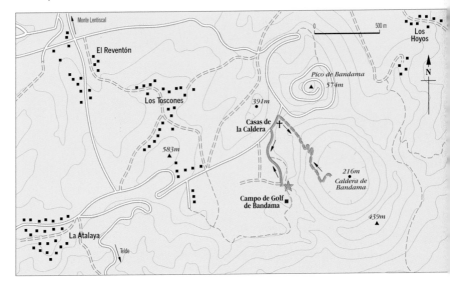

Fuerteventura

Miguel de Unamuno, the Spanish poet and philosopher exiled to Fuerteventura by General Franco, once described the island as 'an oasis in the desert of civilisation'. To the less spiritually inclined, however, Fuerteventura is simply a desert, and a windy one at that. In fact, it is quite possible that the island took its name from the strong wind, *el viento fuerte*, that is a near-permanent feature here.

Gathering fodder is no easy task on the arid island of Fuerteventura

Away from the seductive, sandy beaches – the finest in all the Canaries – is a harsh, arid land, largely devoid of water, trees, or people. Fuerteventura is actually the second largest of all the Canary Islands, bigger than Gran Canaria, yet its entire population of 42,350 would fit into a small suburb of Las Palmas.

In geological terms, Fuerteventura is the oldest of the islands, and it certainly looks the most ancient. Its once sharp volcanic peaks have been worn and weathered by the elements into a series of gentle humps and bumps, which take on a certain splendour at sunset as they bask and glow in warm, ruddy hues. But it would be wrong to suggest that the landscape of Fuerteventura is dull. Many visitors find in it a barren form of grandeur, and the dunes of Corralejo and Jandía are natural wonders of great beauty. Nevertheless, few people come to the island for its sights, or its choice of resorts. The latter are fledgling, and all are relatively low-key. Visitors usually come here for quiet beach holidays to indulge in some of the best windsurfing conditions in the world, or simply to get away from it all.

0   10   20 km

Playa de Barlovento

Punta Pesebre

807m

Cofete   Jandía

Macizo de Jan

Punta de Jandía

Morro Jable   Jandía P

Punta del Mato

Fuerteventura

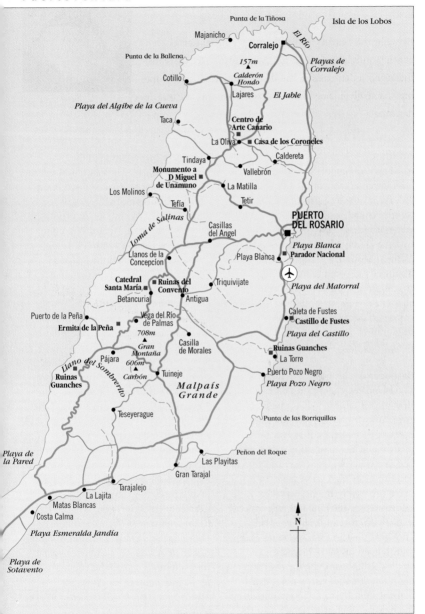

Punta de la Tiñosa

Isla de los Lobos

Majanicho

El Río

Corralejo

Punta de la Ballena

157m
*Calderón
Hondo*

*Playas de
Corralejo*

Cotillo

Lajares

El Jable

Playa del Algibe de la Cueva

Taca

**Centro de
Arte Canario**

La Oliva ■ **Casa de los Coroneles**

Tindaya

Caldereta

**Monumento a
D Miguel
de Unamuno**

Vallebrón

Los Molinos

La Matilla

Tefía

Tetir

Loma de Salinas

Casillas
del Angel

**PUERTO
DEL ROSARIO**

Llanos de la
Concepción

Playa Blanca

Playa Blanca
■ **Parador Nacional**

**Catedral
Santa María**

**Ruinas del
Convento**

Triquivijate

Playa del Matorral

Betancuria

Antigua

Puerto de la Peña

Vega del Río
de Palmas

Caleta de Fustes
■ **Castillo de Fustes**

Ermita de la Peña

708m
▲
*Gran
Montaña*

Playa del Castillo

Casilla
de Morales

Ruinas Guanches
● La Torre

Llano del Sombrerito

Pájara

606m
▲
Carbón

Tuineje

Puerto Pozo Negro

Playa Pozo Negro

**Ruinas
Guanches**

*Malpaís
Grande*

Teseyerague

Punta de las Borriquillas

*Playa de
la Pared*

Peñon del Roque

Las Playitas

Gran Tarajal

N

Tarajalejo

La Lajita

Matas Blancas

Costa Calma

Playa Esmeralda Jandía

*Playa de
Sotavento*

Central Fuerteventura

Between the beaches of north and south is a bare, arid, gently undulating volcanic landscape. A drive to Betancuria, the island's historical and literal oasis, is a must, and there is enough sightseeing here for a leisurely day out.

The windmill at Antigua

Antigua

Although Antigua dates back to 1485, it is an unremarkable but pretty place, redeemed only by a handsome 18th-century church which contains a venerated image.

Some 2km north of the town is the Antiguo Molino, a fine stone windmill, beautifully restored to its pristine condition of some 200 years ago. The adjacent fine granary building has been converted into a popular rustic restaurant.

Restaurant open: daily 10am–6pm.

Betancuria

The island conqueror, Jean de Béthencourt, founded his capital here in 1405, away from the coast, to escape Berber pirate attacks. It enjoys a picturesque location, along a dry river bed in a valley which remains fertile on account of its high water table.

Unfortunately, the Berbers were undeterred by the long trek inland, and in 1539 destroyed the church (also known as the Cathedral of Santa María), and shipped off 600 Christians to slavery. Rebuilt in 1620, the church has a plain interior with naïve-style pastel-painted side altars providing relief from the Baroque high altar. Don't miss the

Judgement Day painting in the southwest chapel. The Church Museum, **Museo de Arte Sacro**, is housed in the ancient former presbytery across the church square. Within its four rooms, the most important treasures are the figure of Santiago (*see* San Bartolomé de Tirajana, *pp42–3*) and the Pendón de la Conquista (Banner of the Conquest), which the islanders believe to be Béthencourt's original flag.

Betancuria continued to be the island's capital until 1834, but today the settlement is little more than a village. Some of its ancient houses date back over five centuries. There is a low-key archaeology museum (Museo Arqueológico) on the other side of the river, where you will also find shops and a local bar-restaurant.

Five minutes' walk north of town (accessible from the main road, but easy to miss) are the picturesque ruins of a Franciscan Convent (Ruinas del Convento) built in 1414.

31km southwest of Puerto del Rosario. Only one person tends the church and the Museo de Arte Sacro, therefore opening times alternate on each half hour and last for half an hour: Open: Mon–Sat 10am–5pm. The church is opened at 5pm only for mass.

Castillo/Caleta de Fustes

This pleasant, low-rise seaside development is based around a golden beach which is safe for children, and culminates in a small pleasure marina. Fishing charters and a diving school operate from here. The eponymous castle is a small, circular 18th-century tower, incorporated pleasantly into an entertainment plaza.
11km south of airport. The castle is not open to the public.

Pájara

This bright and tidy small village is famous for its church Iglesia de la Virgen de la Regla, which dates from 1645–87. Its wooden altars are decorated with simply painted flowers, and there is a coffered ceiling (coin-operated ceiling lights facilitate better viewing). However, it is the church portal which is remarkable – made of soft, pink sandstone, and carved with Aztec-style symbols. It is thought to date from the 16th century, with symbols of suns and snakes, lions and doves, but its origin is a mystery.
15km south of Betancuria.

Tijuene

This is a typical small village where you can see a working windmill producing flour in the windmill centre.
Open: Tue–Sun 9.30am–5pm. Near the centre is a well-kept garden exhibit.
Open: Mon–Sun 10am–6pm.

Vega del Río de Palmas

The literal translation, 'Valley of the River of Palms', spells out the scenic attraction of this oasis area. The Santuario Virgen de la Peña is an atmospheric old church with a statue of the Virgin and a 14th-century confessional. Note the large number of 1920s Aeromotor Chicago Co windpumps still operating around here.
5km south of Betancuria.
Church open: Tue–Sun 11am–1pm & 5–7pm.

The ancient capital of Betancuria is a welcome oasis in the dusty interior

Northern Fuerteventura

A beach of your own –
near Corralejo .

Northern Fuerteventura is a fine place for a family holiday.
Corralejo offers most facilities, including fabulous dunes,
the chance to visit a real desert island, and a day excursion
to Lanzarote. For culture vultures, the excellent modern art
gallery at La Oliva, and the historic charms of Betancuria
(*see p54*) are within easy reach.

Corralejo

This is the most complete
resort on the island, yet it
still manages to retain a
local atmosphere. It
clusters around the fishing
port, with ferries plying to
and from Lanzarote (40
minutes) and Isla de los
Lobos, while children play
on the small, sandy
beaches. The centre is a
small, busy square with a
bandstand, shops, and
tourist restaurants. In the
evenings, you can choose
between a quiet night out
with typical English food
and drink, or you can opt
for local atmosphere with
Spanish guitars, flamenco
dancing, and local food.
Just around the corner are
bars and restaurants. The
10km-long snow-white
beach and dunes lie just
outside town. The dunes,
set against a rugged
mountain backdrop, are
wild and beautiful.
38km north of the airport.

Cotillo

Cotillo is a small, dusty
fishing village on the west
coast, with a handful of
holiday apartments and a
couple of restaurants. It
has a certain 'frontier'
appeal; there is a beach to
the north of the harbour,
colonised by new houses
and apartments, but the
best sands lie a short
distance south (on unmade
roads), past the 17th-
century tower of Castillo
de Rico Roque (not open
to the public). Beware of
offshore winds if
swimming from either
beaches.
*22km southwest of
Corralejo.*

Isla de los Lobos

Los Lobos refers to the
seals (*lobos marinos*) which
once swam off this tiny
island. A good beach, a
drinks shack, natural
beauty, and peace and
quiet are its simple but

THE SPANISH
FOREIGN LEGION

While Spain still
clings onto her
North African territories
of Ceuta and Melilla, it's
likely that Fuerteventura,
the nearest Canarian
territory to Africa, will
remain the base for that
most hard-bitten of all its
armed forces – the
Spanish Foreign Legion. A
mercenary army created
by the French, the Legion
fought mainly in countries
outside France. Spain was
one of them. Their
headquarters is in Puerto
del Rosario, on the
Corralejo road next to the
port. Here, in formal
gardens in front of the
barracks, is a display of
modern weaponry, heroic
statues, and some curious
wooden totem poles.

alluring ingredients. Glass-bottom boats make the trip to the island so that the clear waters may be enjoyed en route. *3km (30-minute) boat trip north of Corralejo. Trips normally depart from Corralejo harbour at 11am, and return from Los Lobos at 5.30pm daily, but do confirm timings. Book through any local travel agent.*

La Oliva

During the 18th century, this village was the joint seat of government with Antigua. Since then, it has fallen on hard times. Its stagnation is summed up by the grandiose, decaying Casa de los Coroneles (House of the Colonels). This 18th-century, 40-room mansion, with fine Canarian balconies, was the house of the islands' military commanders, used up to the middle of the 20th century by Franco's forces.

Another haughty building (also closed to the public) is the parish church, which holds some fine paintings, but is currently undergoing lengthy restoration work. Very definitely open is the new **Centro de Arte Canario**, one of the finest collections of modern Canarian art on the islands. Works range from completely avant-garde to completely accessible, and are well displayed in traditional and modern settings.
La Oliva is 16km south of Corralejo. Centro de Arte Canario. Tel: (928) 868233. Open: Mon–Sat (summer) 10am–6pm, (winter) 10am–5pm. Admission charge.

Puerto del Rosario

Despite its capital status, there's nothing in this town of interest to tourists. Still, you could do worse than browse around the small, tourist-free centre, then enjoy a plate of *el cocido* (the island's meat and chickpea stew) in one of the cafés overlooking the harbour. Ferries run from here to Lanzarote.
30km south of Corralejo. Tourist information: Oficina de Turismo, Avenida de la Constitución 5. Tel: (928) 851400. Open: Mon–Fri 8am–2pm.

The House of the Colonels, La Oliva

Southern Fuerteventura

The south of Fuerteventura can only mean the magnificent beaches of the Jandía peninsula. Along with those of Corralejo, they are rated the best in all the Canaries.

Gran Tarajal/Tarajalejo

Gran Tarajal is the port from which Fuerteventura's high-grade tomatoes are shipped. Next to the port is a black beach with a smart new promenade, and with cafés, restaurants, and lovely tall palm trees.

The former fishing village of Tarajalejo, a few kilometres along the coast, has a similar black beach and resort aspirations. But with the golden sands of Jandía just a short drive south, it's unlikely that either of these resorts will expand beyond a local clientele. *Gran Tarajal and Tarajalejo are 53km and 40km, respectively, northeast of Morro Jable.*

Jandía

The **Playa de Sotavento** ('leeward beach'), which lines the whole south coast of the Jandía peninsula, is the beach which has made Fuerteventura famous. These golden white shores, lapped by ultramarine waters, have launched a thousand postcards and attract the bulk of the island's tourists. There are over 30km to choose from, so it's not difficult to find a patch of your own. The beach varies from pretty coves with low-cliff backing (as at Costa Calma) to magnificent dunes (just south of the landmark Hotel Los Gorriones), as well as great desert-like expanses. Jandía is becoming a very popular resort, which, although having the usual tourist complexes, commercial centres, bars and restaurants, also incorporates a certain degree of individuality and uniqueness in the development. In any case, the beautiful beach more than compensates for the tourist presence. *The northernmost point of the Jandía peninsula, Casas de Matas Blancas, is several kilometres southwest of the airport.*

Las Playitas

Authentic fishing villages are a novelty on Fuerteventura, so it's worth a detour to this attractive little spot, which has been colonised to a lesser extent by a clutch of apartments and bungalows. There's a good (dark) beach and some highly-regarded fish restaurants. *6.5km northeast of Gran Tarajal.*

Morro Jable

This is the southernmost resort of the Jandía peninsula, and the only settlement of any character on this coast. It is built on either side of a *barranco* (ravine), and its erstwhile existence as a fishing village, rather than a tourist centre, means it maintains its 'olde worlde' image. However, many travellers have discovered its fish restaurants. There's a pleasant promenade by the town beach, with a choice of cafés and restaurants. Unless

you have a four-wheel drive vehicle, this is the end of the line. The road south goes no further. A hydrofoil service links Morro Jable to Tenerife.
Southeast of the airport.

Playa de Barlovento

This wild beach (its name means 'windward') on the north coast of the Jandía peninsula is only accessible to four-wheel drive vehicles. Those who do make the effort are rewarded with superb, unspoiled scenery. It's a glorious beach, but the currents here are treacherous and have claimed the lives of several unwary swimmers in recent years.

The only sign of civilisation is the hamlet and bar of Cofete. From here you can see the large, derelict Villa Winter. Gustav Winter, a German engineer, was given this land by General Franco for services rendered. He was also a Nazi sympathiser and it is rumoured that this was a halfway house for war criminals fleeing to South America.
8km north of Jandía.

Rhapsody in blue – the breathtaking shoreline of Playa de Sotavento, on the Jandía peninsula

Windsurfing

Windsurfing is by far the most popular watersport in the Canaries, and the beaches of Sotavento (Jandía, Fuerteventura) and El Médano (Tenerife) draw devotees of the sport from all over the world. The winds don't *always* blow on the islands, however, and the average reliability rate is around 50 per cent in winter and 60–75 per cent in summer. Tenerife is windier than Lanzarote, which is windier than Fuerteventura. However, when it comes to wave-sailing conditions, the order is probably reversed.

The annual world championship speed finals are held at Playa de Sotavento in July and August and, with wind speeds up to force 9, contestants fly across the waves. International Speed Weeks are also held here. The centre of activity is the Procenter F2 school at Los Gorriones hotel.

On the windward (western) side of Fuerteventura conditions can also be thrilling, and Cotillo is a popular spot with experienced windsurfers, but beware – this beach is said to break more kit than any other surf location in Europe! The west side of the island should be treated with great caution, due to treacherous currents.

El Médano, on the east coast of Tenerife, is generally very windy, and is the venue for the World Cup each July. There are two F2 centres here. Playa de las Américas also provides some thrilling and heavy wave-sailing conditions.

On Gran Canaria, speed merchants are well catered for at Maspalomas/ Playa del Inglés, Pozo Izquierdo, and Playa de Vargas, where four-times world champion Björn Dunkerbeck directs the Passat School. Come in summer, when

the southerly tradewinds provide extremely fast conditions.

The Lanzarote Surf Company, at Costa Teguise, is another F2 centre where the surfing reaches epic speeds. Experienced sailors may also like to check out Famara (not for the faint-hearted!) and Jameos del Agua. It's not all thrills and spills, however. If you are just learning, or progressing,

When the going gets tough, the tough get going – cutting the water at El Médano, on Tenerife's east coast

there are several venues throughout the larger islands which provide experienced tuition and calm waters on which to build up confidence and perfect technique (*see p154*). Take all the usual precautions, and bear in mind that there are very few rescue services.

Walk: El Sendero de Bayuyo

CorralejoⷧⷧLajares
FUERTEVENTURA
Puerto
Rosario
Antigua
Gran Tarajal
Morro del Jable

This walk follows an ancient pathway (*sendero*), recently renovated by the island tourism authorities to show something of the volcanic origins and wild landscape of Fuerteventura. An interpretive centre is planned, and its site is marked half-way along the walk. This is an easy trek for all ages and fitness levels, and most of it can be negotiated by a four-wheel drive vehicle. If you can time the walk for sunset you will enjoy the wonderful sight of the landscape bathed in rich velvety reds, browns, and purples. Out of the sun, you may need to wrap up (particularly in winter).

Allow 1½ hours.

For Sendero de Bayuyo, turn off the Lajares road by the Campo de Futbol.

Exactly 1km down the road, the path is marked, next to a house, on the right.

Sand dunes and ancient volcanoes form the Fuerteventura landscape

The walk initially heads straight for the **Montaña Colorada** (Coloured Mountain), an ancient volcano of many hues, then skirts it to the right. Notice the low stone walls dividing the fields; even in this wilderness, crops are grown.

The path climbs slowly, skirting an adjacent volcano, **Calderón Hondo**. The views backwards (south), to the side (east), and forwards (north), sweep across miles of empty countryside, bordered by ancient, softly rounded volcanic cones. After 20 minutes you will see the beach of Corralejo ahead in the distance. After a few minutes, the Isla de los Lobos (right) and Lanzarote (in the far distance) become clear. *Take the fork to the left. After about 30 minutes, the path ascends to the top of Calderón.*

Here, 223m above Corralejo, there is a viewing platform (and safety rails) for looking down into the 8,000-year-old crater. The golden beaches of Playa Blanca and volcanic landscape of Lanzarote are also clearly visible. *Descend the path and continue down to the left.*

Disappointingly, the path ends in a small, scrubby, sandy area. If you have proper walking gear and are feeling adventurous, it is possible to walk right round the volcanoes. If not, simply return along the same path.

A Volcanic Extension
The path of Bayuyo is part of an old trail which connects Corralejo to the interior. This land was created some 8,000 years ago in a series of volcanic eruptions which formed the present northern coast of the island, and also threw up the island of Los Lobos. To continue to Corralejo, take the path leading down to the sea, visible from Calderón Hondo. The last volcano before Corralejo is Bayuyo, the highest of the group. It's an easy climb, and offers the best views north. Allow three hours' walking to get to Corralejo. A short taxi ride (about 10km) will get you back to the start of the route.

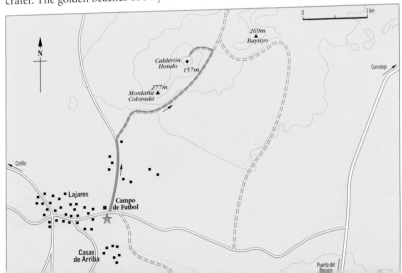

Lanzarote

In any poll of favourite Canary Islands, Lanzarote will always feature near the top. This extraordinary place is, above all, visually striking. Many volcanic islands around the world have black beaches and some have blackened fields, yet none has turned a volcanic catastrophe into such an art form.

Small details enhance the appearance of homes

In back gardens the black ash has been corralled as neatly as any manicured lawn, surrounded by whitewashed stone walls, and planted with hibiscus and bougainvillea. The houses are small and white, with green frames and doors (the island's official colour scheme), and their chimneys are topped with Moorish-style onion domes. In the fields, potatoes, onions, and tomatoes grow on the same volcanic debris. Each group of plants is protected from sun and wind by a semicircular stone wall. As this repeating pattern slopes away to infinity against the blackened mountain slopes, the effect is as hypnotic as any piece of modern art. To add to this are the beautiful beaches of the south, and the unpolluted azure seas around the island.

The Mirador del Río offers one of the Canaries' most spectacular views

Lanzaroteños have long realised the value of their landscape and, in order to preserve it, they have banned all visual distractions. Thus, there are no disfiguring advertising hoardings, no pylons (cables run underground), and there are no high-rise blocks to blot the surroundings.

The man largely responsible for these environmental measures was island hero César Manrique (1919–92). This multi-talented artist and designer also created a series of semi-natural attractions on the island that no visitor should miss (*see also pp68–9*). For all the island's neat and tidy ways, however, the visitor's abiding memory will be of a chaos that no man could have created or mastered. Lanzarote's Mountains of Fire are as convincing a lunar landscape as any on earth, and they offer the ultimate visual thrill on this unique island.

Lanzarote

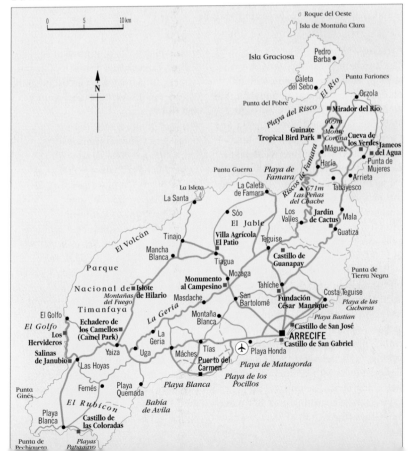

Arrecife and Puerto del Carmen

The only thing that Arrecife and Puerto del Carmen have in common is that they were once small fishing ports. Nowadays, Arrecife is Lanzarote's principal town, while Puerto del Carmen is the principal resort. Neither is large; half the island's total population may live in Arrecife, but that is only 40,000 people, and Puerto del Carmen, though expanding, is still far from becoming the next Playa de las Américas. The most charming parts of each are to be found, inevitably, where the fishing boats lie.

Puerto del Carmen's old port is a picturesque and lively place

Arrecife

The capital of Lanzarote, Arrecife is an absolute haven for shoppers, with its many small craft shops, boutiques, cafés, and restaurants. The main historical attraction is the late 18th-century **Castillo de San José**, restored to hold the acclaimed **Museo Internacional de Arte Contemporáneo** (International Museum of Contemporary Art), which includes works by Picasso and Miró. This lies a short distance out of town, just off the Costa Teguise road. There is a bar and restaurant (*open: 1–3.45 pm, 8–11.30 pm*).

The castle on a small island, just off the seafront near the centre of town, is the **Castillo de San Gabriel**, built in 1590. This now houses a small archaeological museum. The landmark church tower opposite the castle belongs to the **Iglesia de San Ginés**. Restored to its 18th-century glory, it's well worth a visit. Behind it is the capital's most charming spot, **El Charco San Ginés** (the lagoon of San Ginés),

where small boats gently bob at anchor. Bigger boats lie north of here – Arrecife is the island's main fishing port. A ferry service runs to Fuerteventura and Gran Canaria.

6km east of the airport. Tourist information: Parque Municipal (seafront). Tel: (928) 811860/801517. Open: Mon–Fri 10am–1pm & 4.30–7.30pm, Sat 9am–1pm. Castillo de San José, Avenida de Naos: Tel: (928) 812321. Open: daily 11am–9pm. Free admission. Castello de San Gabriel museum: Tel: (928) 802884. Open: Mon–Fri 9am–2.45pm. Free admission. Iglesia de San Ginés: Plaza de San Ginés, off Aquilino Fernández. Open: daily 9am–1pm, 5–7pm, except during services.

Fundación César Manrique (César Manrique Foundation)

This was the home and studio of the late great Lanzarote artist (*see pp68–9*) until 1987, and it was opened to the public in 1992, a few months after his death. Here you can see some of his best works of art and get a preview of the attractions that he has designed on the island. His house is a startling troglodyte vision, though these caves are not man-made, but the result of five volcanic gas bubbles. The landscaping here is a rehearsal for his Jameos del Agua masterpiece (*see p73*). The Foundation has a bookshop, souvenir boutique, snack bar, and parking.

Tahíche, 5km north of Arrecife.
Tel: (928) 843138/843070;
fax: (928) 843463;
www.cesarmanrique.com Open: winter,
Mon–Sat 10am–6pm, Sun 10am–3pm;
summer, daily 10am–7pm.
Admission charge.

Matagorda

This small tranquil resort lies just outside Puerto del Carmen on the road to the airport, and is fast becoming a favourite for all those who like quiet, relaxing holidays.

Playa de las Pocillos

This newly opened beach is considered one of the top ten beaches in Lanzarote. It is very safe for children and offers a quiet, peaceful holiday.

Puerto del Carmen

This is by far the island's largest and busiest resort. The front is heavily commercialised and the César Manrique spirit is lost amid gaudy bars and restaurant fronts. A few metres back, however, peace and quiet return amid low-rise developments. The old part of town survives around the picturesque fishing port, with charming fish restaurants and down-to-earth bars.

For smarter boats, head south to the pretty development of Puerto Calero, which has a pleasure marina.

Puerto del Carmen old town is 10km
southwest of the airport. Tourist
information: Avenida del Playas (seafront,
opp Restaurante Playa Mar). Tel: (928)
813792. Open: Mon–Fri 10am–2pm &
4–7pm, Sat 10am–2pm.

Built on the orders of King Philip II of Spain, the Castillo de San José protects Arrecife's deep-water fishing harbour

César Manrique

The tribute most often paid to César Manrique is that without his efforts tourist development on Lanzarote would have followed the high-rise, high-density route, and the island would have lost its identity. In the environmentally-conscious 21st century, Lanzarote is studied by other countries who are developing tourism, and is used as a role model.

Manrique was born in Arrecife in 1919, and studied art in Madrid and New York at a time when surrealism was a major influence. He returned to his beloved island in 1968, determined to preserve its natural beauty in the face of tourism. His major set-piece visitor attractions, Jameos del Agua (*above*), Mirador del Río, and Jardín de Cactus (*facing page, above*) are masterpieces of design which are totally in harmony with the landscape (*see p73*).

The hallmarks of any Manrique project are the use of local materials, integration with nature, and a completely peaceful atmosphere (often helped by ethereal 'mood music'), all finished with a flourish of his own brand of surreal art.

Manrique was far more than just an artist and designer, however. He was the driving force behind the island's whole tourism development philosophy. He was a fiery orator and a tireless promoter of the island, and it is thanks to him that almost all the architecture on Lanzarote remains in traditional style, and that there is still a total ban on advertising hoardings.

César Manrique died in a car accident just outside his Taro de Tahíche home in September 1992. His influence has been so pervasive throughout Lanzarote that his philosophy is sure to live on.

THE MANRIQUE ROLL CALL

In addition to the projects listed earlier, César Manrique also designed the following island attractions: Monumento al Campesino, Mozaga; Fundación César Manrique, Tahíche; Restaurant El Diablo, and the devil-motif park boundary signs, Montañas del Fuego; Museo Internacional del Arte Contemporáneo, Arrecife; Las Salinas hotel, Costa Teguise; La Era restaurant, Yaiza (conversion and restoration). Look out, too, for his weird and wonderful wind-mobiles around the island.

Manrique's talents are also in evidence on other Canary Islands: Lido Martiánez and Playa Jardín in Puerto de la Cruz, on Tenerife; Mirador de la Peña on El Hierro; Mirador del Palmarejo (still under construction) on La Gomera; Restaurant El Molino near Antigua, on Fuerteventura.

The many creations of Manrique – from landscape design to modern sculpture

Montañas del Fuego

Lanzarote's Montañas del Fuego ('Mountains of Fire') are among the most dramatic landscapes on earth. In fact, the earth will probably be the farthest place from your mind as you view this apocalyptic scene. The brooding craters and scorched, pock-marked land are completely lunar in appearance. Yet, even within these badlands, the locals harvest crops, and on the very edge of the Mountains of Fire, vineyards flourish.

Crops grow from the ashes at La Geria. Low stone walls protect plants from strong winds

El Golfo
The main attraction at El Golfo ('the Gulf') is a small lagoon which, when the light is right, glows a deep emerald green, caused by its algae. Surrounding this is half of the old volcano of El Golfo; the other half has been eaten away by the sea to create a spectacular amphitheatre with a richly coloured cross-section.

The lagoon is not obvious from the main road. Just before you enter the small fishing village of El Golfo (famous for its restaurants), park your car on the hill to the left, and walk the short way around the headland to find it.
12km northwest of Yaiza.

La Geria
La Geria is a valley of black volcanic ash which has been ingeniously cultivated to become Lanzarote's wine region. Vines are planted in shallow depressions, each surrounded by a horseshoe-shaped stone wall, about a metre high. This gives protection from the wind, and helps the lava covering the crop (*see pp74–5*) condense what little moisture

there is. The effect of thousands of these shelters, stretching across the coal-black hillsides, is as startling as any piece of modern art. And despite the apparently barren conditions, each vine can produce up to 200kg of grapes. You can taste the end product at any one of several *bodegas* (wineries), signposted off the Masdache-Uga road, which follows the valley and delineates the region.

Parque Nacional de Timanfaya/Montañas del Fuego
The Mountains of Fire were largely created between 1730 and 1736 by a series of 26 volcanic eruptions which devastated around a quarter of the island and buried 11 villages (*see also pp8–9*). Fortunately there were no casualties, but many Lanzaroteños lost everything, and were forced to emigrate to Gran Canaria. In 1974, the area around the epicentre of this region was declared the National Park of Timanfaya (named after the largest of the volcanoes).

If you approach from the south, the badlands of the Mountains of Fire start just north of Yaiza. You are not allowed to leave your car in this area; it is impossible to walk on the devastated terrain, anyway. Stop at the **Echadero de los Camellos** ('Camel Park'), and you can ride on a dromedary into the volcanic wasteland. The activity here is sometimes frenetic and well worth seeing, although the 10–15-minute ride is really only of novelty value.

A little further on, a ticket kiosk gives access to the **Islote de Hilario**, which is as far into the park as cars are permitted. Here, a guide demonstrates the geothermal energy below your feet: a tube of water is transformed into a scalding geyser, and a dry bush ignites when dropped into a crevice. The restaurant 'El Diablo' here uses the volcano as a giant barbecue.

Included in your ticket price is the 'Route of the Volcanoes' coach tour. This is an unforgettable one-hour tour, with commentary, including a stop at a breathtaking *mirador* right above the fissure line. (If you do this tour as part of a travel package it may not stop at the *mirador* – check before you book.)
(For details of a guided walk in the Mountains of Fire see pp80–81.)
National Park entrance is 7km north of Yaiza. Tel: (928) 840057/840056. Visitors centre: Tel: (928) 840831.
Open: daily 9am–4.45pm (last coach tour). Admission charge. Camel Park is 3km north of Yaiza. Open: daily 9am–5pm.

The Mountains of Fire – still aglow after 260 years of activity

Northern Lanzarote

The north of Lanzarote was unscathed by the 18th-century volcanic devastation of Timanfaya, and so has a less scarred character than the south. Nevertheless, the northern massif is spectacular, and the sculptor César Manrique (*see pp68–9*) has enhanced nature with three outstanding creations.

The labyrinthine Cueva de los Verdes

Cueva de los Verdes

The 'Greens' Cave (which takes its name from previous owners) was created some 5,000 years ago by exploding volcanic gases and lava, creating a labyrinth of tunnels from Monte Corona to the sea. These total some seven kilometres and once provided a refuge from pirates. Nowadays, guides take tourists along two kilometres of the tunnels, ducking and dodging along narrow, often low, atmospherically lit passageways. A memorable trip ends with a brilliant natural optical illusion.

26km north of Arrecife. Tel: (928) 835010. Open: daily 10am–6pm (last tour 6pm). Admission charge.

Haría

Haría is a pristine white village set in the middle of a beautiful, palm-studded valley. Look in at the **Centro Artesanía** (handicraft centre) and **El Museo de Arte Sacro** (Popular Museum of Sacred Popular Art). The best view of the village and valley is to be had from the Mirador de Haría, 4km south, from where it looks like a North African oasis settlement.

The Plaza de la Constitucion, Haría

Some 4km north is the **Guinate Tropical Bird Park**, set on the cliffside. About 300 species are represented here, and parrot shows delight the children.
Haría is 15km northeast of Teguise. Centro Artesanía: Calle Barranco 4. Closed: lunchtime, Mon afternoon & Sun morning. Museo de Arte Sacro (tel: (928) 835009) is adjacent to Iglesia de la Encarnacion. Open: Mon–Fri 11am–1pm & 4–6pm. Admission charge. Guinate Tropical Bird Park: Tel: (928) 835500. Open: daily 10am–5pm. Admission charge.

Isla Graciosa

This small island is just 2km from Lanzarote at its nearest point. There are no cars and no tourist developments – just excellent beaches, a bar-restaurant, and a couple of pensions *(see p139)*.
40-minute daily ferry service from Orzola (35km north of Arrecife). Departs 10am, returns 4pm.

Jameos del Agua

A *jameo* is a subterranean chamber or cave, formed by a volcanic gas bubble, which has lost its roof and is open to the air. This spectacular César Manrique creation uses a series of these chambers to create a fantasy grotto. The first is transformed into a cool restaurant-bar area, luxuriant with tropical plants. A shallow mirror pool leads to a tiny underground lagoon with tiny white albino crabs, usually only found deep in the ocean, and stranded here long ago. As you emerge from the darkness there's a shock in store: an idyllic South Seas beach vision with a tall palm bending over bright blue water. Yet another cave

is used in the evenings on Tuesdays, Fridays, and Saturdays for folk dancing and other entertainments.
27km north of Arrecife. Tel: (928) 848020. Open: daily 9.30am–7pm; Tue, Fri & Sat, also 7pm–3am (folkloric shows). Admission charge.

Jardín de Cactus (Cactus Garden)

Don't be put off by the dry-sounding concept of a cactus garden. This is an inspired piece of landscaping with over 10,000 specimens of all shapes and sizes, interspersed with huge finger-shaped volcanic rocks, reminiscent of a Dalí painting. This was one of César Manrique's last works. He converted an old unused quarry into this impressive cactus plantation.
Guatiza, 17km northeast of Arrecife. Tel: (928) 529397. Open: daily 10am–6pm (winter), till 7pm (summer). Admission charge. The bar and café are open from 10am–5pm.

Mirador del Río

This ancient lookout point is one of the finest *miradores* in all the Canary Islands. It was once used to warn of approaching pirate ships, and in the 1898 Spanish-American war, was a gun battery. César Manrique added curving white walls, picture windows, a balcony, a restaurant, and a bar. From a height of 450m, it descends in an almost sheer drop to reveal the beautiful beaches of Graciosa, and the blue strait of El Río.
9km north of Haría. Tel: (928) 644318. Open: daily 10am–6pm. Admission charge. The bar and café are open from 10am–5pm.

Life on the land has always been particularly hard on the eastern Canary Islands. If the sun does not burn the crops and the wind does not blow them away, a freak gust of locusts, blown across from North Africa, can devour a season's work in minutes. Imagine, then, the feelings of Lanzarote's farmers surveying their fields, covered by a layer of black volcanic ash following the devastating explosions of the 1730s. Imagine, too, their surprise and delight when their crops not only began to grow through the cinders, but were actually healthier than before. The Lanzaroteños soon learned that the porous black *lapilli* or *picon* (pumice particles) helped to soak up what little moisture was in the air, particularly at dusk, and so nourished their plants. This knowledge was passed to the other dry islands, and the spreading of *lapilli* became a common agricultural method on Fuerteventura. Lanzarote's main crops are potatoes, onions, and tomatoes, but vines are also an important produce of the island.

Lanzarote is also still home to the cochineal industry, albeit now on a very minor scale compared with its heyday in the 19th century. Cochineal bugs are raised on prickly pear cacti (originally imported from Mexico), then dried and crushed for the bright red dye which, among other uses, goes to colour aperitifs such as Campari. César Manrique's Jardín de Cactus (see p73), constructed in the cochineal/cactus growing area of Guatiza, is as much of a tribute to Lanzarote's cochineal farmers as his Monumento al Campesino (see p78) is to all Lanzarote's field workers.

On the other islands, bananas have been the main crop since the cochineal demise, yet these too are in decline. Most European buyers reject the small

Canarian bananas (Spain takes over 90 per cent of the crop), but in truth, if you ever eat one, you will never want one from anywhere else, as their taste is unbeatable! Exotic fruits, such as papayas and avocados, and cut flowers are now beginning to replace some banana fields as farmers diversify, but acre upon acre of dark green plantations are still the major feature on the northern coasts of Gran Canaria and the western islands.

In spite of the odds they face, farmers manage to eke out an existence from the land in Fuerteventura and Lanzarote

Southern Lanzarote

The southern peninsula of Lanzarote is topographically the least interesting part of the island. However, for those who brave the rough, unsigned tracks beyond Playa Blanca, the prize is some of the best beaches in the archipelago.

An onion farmer sorts his crop

Femés

This small hamlet is perched on a spectacularly sited saddle between the mountains overlooking Playa Blanca, and is by far the most scenic way to approach the beaches. Stop here on your way back to watch the sun set, colouring the Mountains of Fire in dusky reds and purples. The church of Femés is one of the oldest on the island.

8km northeast of Playa Blanca.

Playa Blanca

The old fishing village of Playa Blanca has been submerged under a new resort which is growing fast. There are two main centres of activity. The largest and more mature is just east of the Fuerteventura ferry terminal. A pleasant promenade with bars and restaurants overlooks the main town beach and Playa Dorado, which is a 15-minute walk away. There is another, smaller, though no less pleasant beach on the other side of the port, known as Playa Flamingo. Both of these beaches soon become full, however, encouraging sun-worshippers to head for Playa Blanca's famous Papagayo ('parrot') beaches. These begin 5km to the east of the resort, and comprise three distinct beaches: Playa de Mujeres, Playa

Papagayo, and Puerto Muelas (also known as La Caleta).

There is one sign to these golden sands, and then the asphalt road disintegrates into a maze of bumpy, dusty dirt tracks. Carloads of people, looking puzzled, frustrated, and simply driving in circles are a common sight just east of Playa Blanca! Many park by the landmark round tower of Castillo de las Coloradas (built in 1769), and make the 25-minute walk to Playa de Mujeres. The only foolproof method of reaching it is to follow someone who knows the way – which is not difficult, as these beaches are very popular.

Having arrived, you will find golden sandy coves with picturesque cliff backings. Playa Papagayo is prettiest of all, and is the only one with a bar-restaurant, although itinerant drinks vendors service the other beaches. Puerto Muelas is popular with nudists.

Playa Blanca is 35km southwest of the airport.

Salinas de Janubio

The saltpans (or saltflats) of Janubio service one of the island's oldest industries, producing salt for the fish processing plants of Arrecife. On a bright day the chequer-board effect of the individual pans, where the seawater evaporates to leave gleaming white squares, is yet another of the island's natural art works. Another spectacle is provided 3km north by **Los Hervideros** ('the boiling springs') where, in rough weather, waves break violently, and spout up through volcanic sea caves. *Salinas de Janubio is 9km north of Playa Blanca.*

Yaiza

Yaiza is usually regarded as the prettiest village on Lanzarote – a neat and tidy collection of old, whitewashed houses with charming floral gardens. The most popular place in the village, the Restaurant La Era, contains one of only three houses which were left standing in Yaiza after the cataclysmic events of 1730–6 (*see p70*). César Manrique (*see pp68–9*) renovated the house, extended it, and converted it into a restaurant in

The almost clinical neatness of the houses of Yaiza, whitewashed to repel the heat of the sun

1970. Do look in, whether or not you intend dining (there is a separate bar area). Also in Yaiza is a fine old 18th-century church, a good private art gallery, and a Casa de Cultura (Cultural Centre), which also provides art exhibition space (but does not keep its stated opening hours).
15km north of Playa Blanca.

Large-scale commercial saltpans at Janubio

Teguise

The town of Teguise is the historic showcase of Lanzarote, with many fine examples of colonial architecture. But life for the island's peasants was (and still is) unrelenting. This is well illustrated by some of the other visitor attractions in this area.

The windmill and wine press at the Villa Agrícola el Patio

Casa Museo/Monumento al Campesino (Museum/Monument to the Field Worker)

César Manrique's tribute to Lanzarote's long-suffering farmers takes the surreal shape of a 15-m high glistening, white tower of blocks which is said to represent the farmer, his cat, and a rat. Symbolically, it is placed in the exact centre of the island. Next to it, Manrique designed a traditional farmhouse which holds a restaurant, a small museum (where artisans often give craft demonstrations), and a shop selling local produce.

Mozaga, 8km northwest of Arrecife. Tel: (928) 520136. Open: daily 10am–6pm. Free admission.

Castillo de Santa Bárbara

High on the old volcano of Guanapay, this golden-coloured castle was built in the 16th century to protect the people of Teguise against pirates. Today it houses the **Museo del Emigrante Canario** (Museum of the Canarian Emigrant), which relates the sad history of mass emigration by Canarian families to South America. The views from here, however, are superb.

1km northeast of Teguise. Tel: (928) 811950. Open: Mon–Fri

10am–5pm, weekends 10am–4pm (in winter it closes one hour earlier). Admission charge.

Costa Teguise

This large, new, up-market *urbanización* (development) is built around an excellent sandy beach. Watersport facilities are good, and there is an 18-hole golf course and aquapark on site.

7km northeast of Arrecife.

Teguise

Teguise is the oldest town on the island, founded in the 15th century, and was the capital until 1852. There are dozens of old buildings to admire, many beautifully restored, in the peaceful atmosphere which cloaks the town six days of the week. On each Sunday, pandemonium breaks out as half the island population and most of its tourists descend on the Sunday market (*see p143*).

The main square is dominated by the great bulk of the **Iglesia de Nuestra Señora de Guadalupe** (Church of Our Lady of Guadalupe), also known as the Iglesia de San Miguel. This was built in the 15th century, but ravaged by pirates in the late-16th and early-17th centuries, and badly fire-damaged in 1909. Opposite is the town's finest historic house, the **Palacio de Spinola**, now converted into a museum. Here you can see how a wealthy 18th-century Genoese merchant family lived. Two other ancient buildings on the square which are open to the public are the Caja de Canarios (Canaries savings bank), which occupies the 15th-century tithe barn, and the Restaurant Acatife, also located in an old mansion.

Adjacent to the main square is the charming Plaza 18 de Julio. The **Centro Natural** (*see p145*) occupies the old hospital building, dating from 1473. In the top left corner of the square (facing the pretty statue of a girl with a pitcher) is the snowy-white Casa Cuartel. This 17th-century balconied house was formerly the local army barracks.

At the top end of town is the handsome 16th-century Convento de San Francisco and the castle of Castillo de Santa Bárbara.
9km north of Arrecife. Palacio de Spinola museum. Tel: (928) 845181. Open: Mon–Fri 9am–3pm, weekends 9.30am–2pm. Admission charge.

Villa Agrícola el Patio

This small group of old agricultural buildings has been beautifully restored to illustrate life on the land between 50 and 100 years ago. An enthusiastic guide (speaking Spanish only) will show you into a windmill, a great barn converted to a museum, a *bodega* (wine store), and outhouses with various types of hand-powered mills. To end the tour, you will be given a taste of local wine, cheese, and breadsticks in an atmospheric bar area.
Tiagua (Sóo road), 12km northwest of Arrecife. Tel: (928) 529134. Open: Mon–Fri 10am–5pm, Sat 10am–2pm. Admission charge.

The main square and the ancient church of historic Teguise

Walk: Fields of Fire

This extraordinary walk through the Parque Nacional de Timanfaya is the perfect complement to the spectacular 'Route of the Volcanoes' coach tour (*see p71*). It may only be undertaken with a guide from ICONA, the Spanish Nature Conservancy body (*see p139*), and must be booked in advance (*tel: (928) 840238/40*). There is no charge for this tour, and anyone who is reasonably active may join it. *Allow total time, including 30 minutes' vehicle transportation, of around 3 hours.*

Start at the Camel Park Geology Museum.

Camel Park Geology Museum

This small museum provides an introduction to the cataclysmic events of 1730–36 which shaped the terrain you are about to cross.
From here you will be transported to the start of the walk, just north of Yaiza, by ICONA minibus.

Tremesana

The walk starts alongside the volcano of Tremesana. This predates the 18th-century eruptions, and vegetation has started to reclaim its slopes. Tremesana is just below Montaña Rajada, on top of which is the spectacular *mirador* visited on the park's own 'Route of the Volcanoes' coach tour. Note the fig trees growing in the stone half-circles which protect the crops from wind. Even here, near the epicentre of the destruction, it is possible to grow crops. One particular stone half-circle is unique, cleverly buttressed to stop it sliding down the mountain. Look for it on the side of

Tremesana. Your guide will also show you a fig-drying circle.
The walk continues alongside the fissure.

Fissure Line

From the *mirador* you will have had an eagle's eye view of this great rent in the earth which runs from Montaña Rajada to Montaña Encantada, caused by the exploding magma. En route you will learn about different types of lava, and the flora and fauna that eke out an existence in the National Park. You may see a locust blown over from Africa, a rabbit, a hawk, or raven, or perhaps even the park's nesting vultures.

The Lava Lake

Lava, gushing forth from the great tear in the earth at up to 70kph, formed a lake (long-since dry) some 5m deep at this point. Peer down into the fissures which reach to the bottom.

Volcanic Tubes

Volcanic gases and lava running underground have formed countless tunnels just below the surface of Lanzarote. Your guide will point out where these occur (from telltale signs such as yellow sulphur stains), and if he is sure that it is safe to do so, may invite the group to jump up and down on the spot to hear the hollow sound from beneath. The most famous volcanic chambers have been converted into living and exhibition spaces at the Fundación César Manrique (*see pp66–7*), but here you can visit two caves in their natural state. One of these was used in the filming of *One Million Years BC*, and your guide will take great delight in showing you the heroine Raquel Welch's cave!

The walk continues for another 10 minutes, past a quarry, to where the ICONA minibus will collect and return you to the Camel Park.

The view from Montaña Rajada of the path of devastation taken by the lava when the volcano erupted. The first explosion occurred on the evening of 1 September 1730 and lasted 19 days. Volcanic activity continued for six years

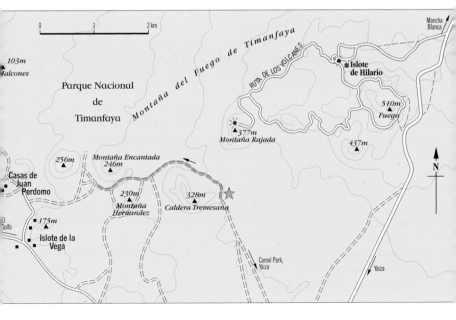

Tenerife

Tenerife is the largest Canary Island, and in Mount Teide boasts the highest point in all Spanish territory. Consequently, the weather contrasts here are greater than on any other island. In winter, the wind may whistle and snow may drift around Mount Teide, while just 40km to the south, sunbathers bronze themselves on the beach.

The south of the island is hot, dry, and arid, with little of sightseeing interest. Its resorts are the brash new face of Tenerife. For history, culture, and scenery you have to go to the north to the fine old colonial towns of La Laguna, La Orotava, and the capital, Santa Cruz. Even Puerto de la Cruz, where tourism on Tenerife was born around a century ago, still retains much of its old character, despite its increasing number of high-rise hotels.

The north is green and lush, which, of course, means rain. It's short, sharp, and only occasional in summer, but in winter it's almost guaranteed to shave a few days off a two-week stay.

Teide rises above everything on Tenerife. The volcanic scenery of its national park is out of this world, but there are plenty of other competing attractions on the island. Zoos, gardens, banana plantations, and museums mean no one need ever be at a loose end here.

Surprisingly, the only thing that Tenerife is short on is good beaches. Only the golden strip of Playa de las Teresitas (near Santa Cruz) is worth a postcard home. However, with alternatives such as the Lido at Puerto de la Cruz and Aguapark Octopus at Playa de las Américas, few people seem to mind.

Tenerife

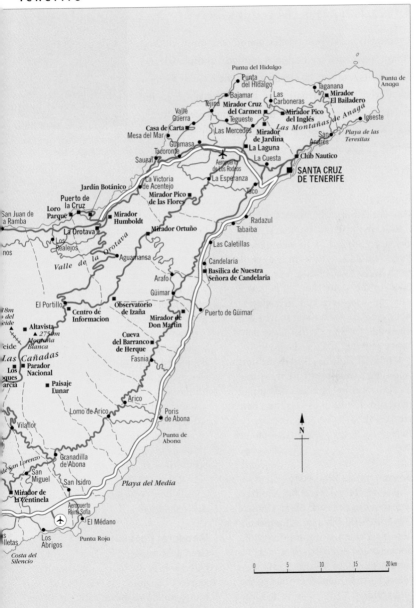

Punta del Hidalgo

Punta de Anaga

Punta del Hidalgo

Taganana
Mirador
El Bailadero

Bajamar
Las Carboneras

Tejina
Mirador Cruz
del Carmen

Mirador Pico
del Inglés

Valle Güerra

Teguesta

Las Montañas de Anaga

Igueste

Casa de Carta

Las Mercedes

Mesa del Mar

San Andres

Playa de las Teresitas

Guamasa
Mirador
de Jardina

Tacoronte
La Laguna

Sauzal
La Cuesta

Club Nautico

Aeropuerto de Los Rodeos

SANTA CRUZ DE TENERIFE

La Victoria de Acentejo

La Esperanza

Taco

Jardín Botánico

Mirador Pico de las Flores

Puerto de la Cruz

Loro Parque

Mirador Humboldt

Radazul

San Juan de la Ramba

La Orotava

Mirador Ortuño

Tabaiba

Los Realejos

Las Caletillas

Valle de la Orotava

Aguamansa

Candelaria

Basílica de Nuestra Señora de Candelaria

Arafo

Güimar

El Portillo
Centro de Informacion

Observatorio de Izaña

Puerto de Güimar

18m del eide

Altavista
▲ 2750m
Montaña Blanca

Mirador de Don Martin

eide

Las Cañadas

Cueva del Barranco de Herque

Los gues arcia

Parador Nacional

Fasnia

Paisaje Lunar

Arico

Lomo de Arico

Poris de Abona

Vilaflor

Punta de Abona

N

de San Lorenzo

Granadilla de Abona

San Miguel

San Isidro

Playa del Media

Mirador de la Centinela

Aeropuerto Reina Sofia

El Médano

lletas
Los Abrigos

Punta Roja

Costa del Silencio

0   5   10   15   20 km

The Anaga Mountains

Despite its great beauty, the panoramic, green-cloaked Anaga Mountains region is still relatively unexplored, and small villages, cut off from the main roads, form a genuinely 'hidden Tenerife'. It is an excellent area for walking, and this is the only way to do it justice. However, it's also an easy area to tour by car, with several fine *miradores* guaranteeing a memorable trip.

Taganana village tumbles down the hillside

Bajamar

Bajamar is one of the oldest tourist resorts on the island, popular with German visitors. Like its fellow veteran, Puerto de la Cruz, it has only a small, black beach to offer its guests, and so the pools by the promenade are popularly used for swimming. Unlike Puerto, however, Bajamar has not moved with the times, and has a rather tired, dated look about it.

Punta del Hidalgo, 3km to the north, is its newer sister resort. Many of the hotels here enjoy excellent cliff-top positions. The sunset views from here are said to be the best on Tenerife. *Bajamar is 30km northeast of Puerto de la Cruz.*

Bosque de las Mercedes

This is a primeval laurel forest, of the type that can be found on La Gomera (*see pp108–11*). This sort of vegetation is now quite rare and much prized by botanists and ecologists. It stretches from north of the village of Las Mercedes to the higher ground of the mountains.
Las Mercedes is 4km north of La Laguna.

Casa de Carta

The beautiful 18th-century Canarian house of the Carta family houses the islands' finest ethnographic collection. The house itself is a superlative example of Canarian architecture with an equally outstanding collection of porticoes, patios, and richly carved woodwork. Its most colourful exhibits are traditional Canarian costumes, which range from the 18th century to the present day. You can see how these were made in the weaving and needlework rooms.

Other displays include reconstructions of various rooms, and a ceramics collection.
Tacoronte–Valle de Guerra Rd, 25km northeast of Puerto de la Cruz.
Tel: (922) 543053. Open: daily 10am–1pm, 3–6pm (winter), 4–7pm (summer). Admission charge.

Miradores (lookout points)
Cruz del Carmen

Fine views to the mountains (north) and to La Laguna and Teide (south) can be enjoyed from this elevation of 920m. An early 17th-century chapel here holds

the much-venerated figure of Nuestra Señora de las Mercedes.
8km northeast of La Laguna.

De Jardina
This is the closest *mirador* to La Laguna, and has a splendid view into the fertile 'garden' area which makes up the city hinterland, and beyond to the east coast.
7km northeast of La Laguna.

El Bailadero
A spectacular viewpoint, perched on a knife-edge of rock, gives a 360-degree view. The town straggling down to the north coast directly below is Taganana.
19km northeast of La Laguna.

Pico del Inglés
One explanation for this curious name ('Peak of the English') is that, in the days of Raleigh and Hawkins, English spies sent signals from here to their marauding ships down below whenever a Spanish galleon was sighted. It is the loftiest (992m) and the best of all the Anaga vantage points, with a striking panorama of the mountains, and (on a clear day) views as far south as Gran Canaria.
9km northeast of La Laguna.

Taganana
This pretty white village is strung out along the hillside, which plunges steeply towards the coast. There are beaches just 2km further north, but these are not suitable for swimming due to their dangerous undertow.
24km northeast of La Laguna.

The Anaga foothills, seen from the Mirador de Jardina (looking south)

La Laguna

La Laguna (officially San Cristóbal de la Laguna) was founded in 1496 by the island conqueror, Alonso Fernández de Lugo as capital of all the Canaries. It remained the main city until the early-18th century, and its numerous handsome 16th- and 17th-century mansions attest to the wealth of this era. Despite its wonderful architecture and Spanish atmosphere, it is almost untouched by tourism. Today, it is the most important town on the island after Santa Cruz, and its university gives it a youthful air in spite of its antiquity.

Ancient houses on Calle San Agustín

Sightseeing here is easy. Start in the unmissable main square of Plaza del Adelantado at the *ayuntamiento* (town hall), where you should be able to pick up a town map. Walk up Calle Obispo Rey Redondo, then return via the parallel street of Calle San Agustín.

The imposing Cathedral of Santa Iglesia

Calle Obispo Rey Redondo

This ancient street possesses many fine buildings. Aside from the Casa de los Capitanes, the Cathedral and the Iglesia de la Nuestra Señora de la Concepción, look out for the **Teatro Leal**, an overbearing pink and yellow confection with two bright red cupolas dating from 1915. Near the top of the street is the charming Plaza de la Concepción, where lovely old houses look onto a square with two dragon trees, and a bizarre Art Nouveau structure covering an electricity substation.

Calle San Agustín

Walking towards the Plaza del Adelantado, look out for the following highlights on this most handsome of streets: **Instituto Cabrera Pinto**, a fine 16th-century ex-convent building with a graceful bell tower; **Palacio Episcopal** (Bishop's Palace), a 17th-century palace with a beautiful patio open to the public (*daily 9am–1pm and 4–6pm*); **Museu de Historia** and **Consejo**

Consultivo de Canarias, No. 16 – peep inside to see the perfect patio of this 1746 house.

Casa de los Capitanes (House of the Captains)

This splendid former residence of the island's Captain Generals dates back some 250 years. It is now part of the town hall and is open to the public during office hours. Go upstairs to see its splendid wooden panelling and its Moorish wooden-trellised oriel window.
Calle Obispo Rey Redondo. Tel: (922) 261011/631965. Open: 9am–1pm & 4–7pm. Free admission.

La Laguna's Historical Museum is the finest in the Canaries

Catedral (Cathedral)

A cavernous, awe-inspiring church, founded in 1515, but remodelled in 1904–5. There are many treasures to admire, and behind the High Altar is the simple tomb of de Lugo.
Plaza Fray Albino, off Calle Obispo Rey Redondo. Tel: (922) 258939. Open: Mon–Sat 8am–1.30pm & 5–7.30pm.

Iglesia de Nuestra Señora de la Concepción (Church of Our Lady of the Conception)

This splendid church is the oldest in La Laguna, built in 1502. It has changed little over the centuries, and its woodwork, particularly the ceiling, shows outstanding craftsmanship.
Calle Obispo Rey Redondo. Tel: (922) 261913. Open: Mon–Fri 10am–noon.

Museu de Historia de Tenerife

This museum charts the history of the island from the Conquest to the present day with a series of well-displayed exhibits. The star attraction is the building itself, the Casa de Lercaro, built in 1593.
Lercaro House, Calle San Agustín 22. Tel: (922) 630121. Open: Tue–Sat 10am–5pm. Admission charge.

Plaza del Adelantado

This is probably the best architectural ensemble in the archipelago. Start at the Neo-Classical 19th-century *ayuntamiento* (top left-hand corner). To the right is the **Convent of Santa Catalina**, with an unusual lattice-work gallery. Adjacent is the **Palacio de Nava**, a colonial Baroque palace. On the opposite side of the square, the **Mercado Municipal** also has a latticed gallery. Next to it is the charming, tiny **Ermita de San Miguel**, built in 1507 by order of Lugo. It's now an exhibition hall.
Convent of Santa Catalina. Open: Mon–Sat 4–6pm, Sun 10am–noon & 4–6pm. Free admission.

La Orotava

La Orotava is a beautifully preserved old colonial town of steep, cobbled streets. Most visitors go only to the showpiece Casas de los Balcones; the rest of town is virtually untouched by tourism. La Orotava is also the craft centre of Tenerife. The finest view of town and the best place to start exploring is in the raised balcony-like Plaza de la Constitución; everything is within five to ten minutes' walk of here.

Plaza de Franco, scene of La Orotava's famous Corpus Christi flower carpets celebrations

Casas de los Balcones (Houses of the Balconies)

This is the quintessential colonial Canarian building, named after the superbly crafted balconies which look onto the courtyard within. The tropical patio, full of exotic greenery, an ancient wine press, old pictures and pottery, conjures up an evocative atmosphere of early colonial days. The houses, joined together, date from the 1630s and, as you can see from an upper-floor museum, were home to a wealthy family. The rest of the building is a craft and souvenir shop, popular for its traditionally dressed embroiderers, and its 'sand-painting' demonstrations. The Casa de Turista, opposite, is similar in style and age, built in 1590. It, too, is a craft and gift shop.
Calle San Francisco. Tel: (922) 382855. Open: Mon–Fri 8.30am–7.00pm, Sat 8.30am–6.30pm. Free admission.

Casa Torrehermosa

This is the official Empresa Insular de Artesanía (island enterprise craft workshop), and it, too, is based in an ancient colonial house, together with a small museum of island crafts.

Next door, in the **Convento de Santo Domingo**, is the modest **Museo de Artesanía Iberoamericana** (Museum of Spanish-American Crafts).
Calle Tomás Zerolo. Tel: (922) 322906. Open: Mon–Fri 9.30am–6pm, Sat 9.30am–2pm. Admission charge. Convento: check notice on door for opening times.

Hijuela del Botánico

The name of this garden, 'Daughter of the Botanic Garden', explains its relationship with its famous 'parent' nearby in Puerto de la Cruz (*see pp96–7*). It is a small, densely planted area claiming over 3,000 different tropical and subtropical species.
Calle Hermano Apolinar. Open: daily dawn–dusk. Free admission.

Hospital de la Santísima Trinidad (Hospital of the Holy Trinity)

Formerly an 18th-century convent, this is now a hospital which cares for mentally handicapped patients. The revolving drum set into the main door was used to donate gifts anonymously.

The view from the hospital terrace over the Orotava Valley is still one of the great sights of this region, though marred by urban development.
Calle San Francisco. Tel: (922) 321633. Open: Mon–Sat 4–5.30pm, Sun 10.30am–noon. Free admission.

Iglesia de Nuestra Señora de la Concepción (Church of Our Lady of the Conception)
Along with its namesake in La Laguna, this is probably one of the finest churches on the island. It is an extravagant, handsome, Baroque structure with twin onion-topped towers and a large yellow dome, built between 1768 and 1788. Its screen, altar, statuary, and carved choir stalls are regarded as masterpieces.
Plaza Casañas. Tel: (922) 330187. Open: usually for mass only.

OROTAVA ENVIRONS
Museo de Cerámica (Pottery Museum)
A collection of around 1,000 pieces of pottery is held in this typical (though much-restored) early 17th-century house. Potters give demonstrations.
La Luz–Las Candias Rd, 2km west of La Orotava. Tel: (922) 333396. Open: Mon–Sat 10am–6pm. Admission charge. Bus: free from Playa Martiánez, Puerto de la Cruz.

The symmetrical elegance of a traditional Canarian balcony, La Orotava

Parque Nacional del Teide

Mount Teide is, at 3,718m, the highlight of Tenerife in every sense, with a dramatic volcanic landscape unrivalled in the Eastern Canary islands. Conditions in the national park vary dramatically. In winter, snow falls, gale-force winds blow, and the roads are sometimes closed. In summer, even this arid landscape is aglow with plants and flowers, and daytime temperatures can soar above 40°C (although the summit of Teide is still chilly). Your journey from the coast may mostly be in the clouds, but just before you arrive at the cable car, these will roll back to reveal bright blue skies and the omnipresent mountain.

A LITTLE HISTORY

About three million years ago, a giant volcano near the present Mount Teide (but much, much bigger) exploded and/or collapsed in on itself. The volcano walls, or what was left of them, formed a *caldera* (crater) in which Teide and other volcanoes now stand. The *caldera* measures 48km in circumference, and some parts of the wall still stand up to 500m high. It may be impossible to visualise this from ground level, but as you gaze upon the torn and twisted earth, try to imagine the awesome power that turned the earth into this alien lunarscape.

El Portillo Visitors Information Centre

The El Portillo office, at the eastern entrance to the national park, offers a small exhibition and information area. You can join a walking tour here, free of charge, with an ICONA guide (*see p139*). Telephone ahead to book your place. If you intend walking on your own, you should still call in here for maps and advice. Walking in the park can be dangerous in winter.
32km south of Puerto de la Cruz. Open: daily 9.30am–4pm. Tel (ICONA Santa Cruz office): (922) 290129/290183. Fax: (922) 244788.

El Teleférico (Cable Car)

Unless you are a keen hill climber, this is the only way to get near the summit of Teide. The car ascends from an altitude of 2,356m to 3,555m in eight minutes. The remaining walk, some 163m to the top, may only be undertaken with a guide. At the summit is an iron cross, a sulphurous smell, and (on a clear day), views of all the other islands and sometimes North Africa.

Note: the car does not operate when it is too windy (which is frequently the case in winter), and in summer there can often be long queues.

43km south of Puerto de la Cruz.
Tel: (922) 383711/383740/694038. The
car operates daily (weather permitting),
9am–4pm.

Los Roques de García
(The Rocks of García)

Los Roques is probably the most
spectacular grouping of pyroclastic
debris within the park, and certainly the
best within easy access of the road. It is
on every coach tour itinerary, and the
rocks are often swarming with day-
trippers. It would be hard to detract
from such a magnificent sight as this,

with views to Teide on one side and, on
the other, the great flat expanse of the
Llano (plain) de Ucanca. This is one of
the park's many *cañadas* – yellow
sedimentary plains where fine debris has
accumulated.

Across the road from Los Roques is
the recently renovated Parador de
Cañadas del Teide.

Close to Los Roques, heading south,
is the rock formation known as Los
Azulejos (*azulejos* are glazed tiles),
where the rocks glint green with iron
hydrate deposits.

47km south of Puerto de la Cruz.

The dramatic formations of Los Roques, with the gullied slopes of Mount Teide in the background

There are nearly 2,000 different species of plants in the Canary Islands, of which around 700 are endemic (exclusive to the islands). Many are only of interest to botanists, but the species mentioned below are all quite remarkable, and can usually be seen without ever having to leave the beaten track.

The biggest and most famous inhabitant of the islands is the dragon tree. A peculiarity of this tree is its lack of rings, which means that telling its age is very difficult. The largest and oldest tree, the Drago Milenario (at Icod de los Vinos, Tenerife), is between 500 and 3,000 years old. Guanches attributed magical properties to the tree and used its 'dragon's blood' sap (which turns red in the air) to heal wounds.

Other strange Canarian trees are the twisted and dead-looking *sabinas* (junipers) of El Hierro, while the protected *laurasilva* laurel forest of La Gomera is a wet, dark, spooky place to explore. By way of contrast, the tall, light, graceful Canary Pine is found on higher ground on all the western islands and Gran Canaria. The endemic tree of the dry eastern islands is the Canary date palm (which does not produce fruit), a close relative of the North African variety. Flora that do bear a harvest are the banana plant and the almond tree, both of which are imports.

The prettiest plants on the islands – bougainvillea, hibiscus, poinsettia, and the graceful *strelitzia* (bird-of-paradise flower) – have also been brought here from other countries.

The largest and most striking endemic flower is the slender red viper's bugloss or *tajinaste* (*Echium wildpretii*), which grows up to 2m high in the Cañadas del Teide park. Also here (and in many other places) is the yellow or white *retama*, or Teide broom, which gives off a wonderful, pungent-sweet scent.

The most noticeable plants of the drier regions are the New World cacti, prickly pears, imported to attract cochineal bugs (*see pp74–5*), and the endemic cactus-like *cardón* (*Euphorbia canariensis*). This is a candelabra spurge with tall, smooth stems (like organ pipes in appearance), very common in the south of Gran Canaria. Other succulents include several species of *senecios* and *tabaibas* – small spiky plants, resembling

yucca trees, which are very tenacious, and soon colonise deserted house roofs.

Facing page, above: *strelitzias* (bird-of-paradise); below: the famous 3,000-year-old dragon tree of Icod de los Vinos (Tenerife). This page, above: a prickle of cacti; orchids in the sub-tropical Palmitos Parque at Maspalomas (Gran Canaria)

Masca's dramatic site
attracts many visitors

Northwestern Tenerife

The northwest corner of Tenerife is a highly rewarding area for exploration. The countryside of the Teno Hills is as beautiful as any scenery to the northeast, and Garachico and Icod de los Vinos are two of the island's most charming small towns.

Garachico

This modest fishing port hides an outstanding collection of ancient buildings among its narrow, cobbled streets. Yet, in 1706, it was all but destroyed by lava flowing down to the sea. To appreciate how Garachico was rebuilt on the lava peninsula that formed here, approach it on the C820 from Icod de los Vinos. As you descend the hillside via El Tanque, you will get a splendid bird's-eye view.

The most notable survivor of the disaster is the beautifully preserved

Garachico offered the best harbour on Tenerife's north coast until it was engulfed by lava in 1706

seafront **Castillo de San Miguel** (Castle of St Michael), which dates from the 16th century. It now houses a small museum of fossils and shells.

Nearby is the port, which until 1706 was the most important in Tenerife because of its fine natural harbour. On the town side is a charming square with a beautiful sunken garden. A 16th-century arch and a 17th-century wine press adorn this flower-filled space. From here there is a view of the 18th-century **Iglesia de Santa Ana** (Church of St Anna).

The town's most beautiful church is the 16th-century **Iglesia de San Francisco** (Church of St Francis) in the adjacent square. The old convent next door now houses a cultural centre, **Casa de Cultura**. At the other end of town is the 17th-century Convento de Santo Domingo, now home to the **Museo de Arte Contemporaneo** (Museum of Contemporary Art).

Garachico is 31km west of Puerto de la Cruz (via El Tanque). Castillo de San Miguel museum tel: (922) 830000. Open: daily 9am–6pm. Admission charge. Casa de Cultura, Plaza de San Francisco tel: (922) 830000. Open: Mon–Fri 9am–7pm, Sat 9am–6pm, Sun 9am–1pm. Museo de Arte Contemporaneo, Plaza

Puerto de Santiago and the Los Gigantes sea cliffs

Santo Domingo tel:(922) 830000.
Open: daily 9am–1pm & 4–7pm.
Admission charge.

Icod de los Vinos

Icod de los Vinos is famous for its 1,000-year-old dragon tree (*Drago Milenario*). The real age of this monster is not known, but it is the oldest dragon tree in existence and, at over 16m tall and with a girth of 6m, it is also the largest.

The classic view of the tree is from the Plaza de la Iglesia, which boasts fine exotic greenery of its own, and hosts the beautiful 15th- to 16th-century Iglesia de San Marcos (Church of St Mark). An even more scenic view from below includes a typical Canarian balcony.
20km west of Puerto de la Cruz.

Los Gigantes/Puerto de Santiago

A quiet, low-rise, up-market holiday development has sprung up here to take advantage of the dramatic sea-cliff setting of Los Gigantes, and the black sandy beach next to Puerto de Santiago. Massive cliffs drop almost sheer into the sea from a height of 500m.
42km north of Playa de las Américas.

Masca

The tip of the northwest is covered by the Teno Hills – one of the most picturesque corners of the island, rent by deep ravines, and cloaked in lush greenery. The road south from Buenavista del Norte passes along steep, narrow hairpin-bends, and leads to the village of Masca. Until recently it was virtually 'undiscovered', but now Masca is on most coach excursion itineraries. Despite the occasional crowds, however, its magical site cannot be diminished. Its houses are set on narrow ridges which plunge down into a verdant valley of dramatic rock formations.
20km southwest of Garachico via Buenavista del Norte.

Marine flippery at the new
dolphinarium, Loro Parque

Puerto de la Cruz

Puerto de la Cruz, or Puerto, as it is known, is the longest
established, and most complete holiday resort on Tenerife.
It has a magnificent backdrop, with Teide towering above,
and the lush Orotava Valley sweeping down to the city.

Unlike most Canarian resorts, this is a
town with its own identity, where locals
still live, work, eat and drink. The
British put Puerto on the map as a
holiday destination around a century
ago, and so it has stayed. In addition to
its old-world charms, such as the 17th-
century Customs House and the
pedestrian promenade at St Telmo
which shouldn't be missed, it also
features some high-quality visitor
attractions on its outskirts.
*Puerto de la Cruz is 60km northwest of
Reina Sofía airport. Tourist office: Plaza
de la Iglesia 3. Tel: (922) 386000. Open:
Mon–Fri 9am–8pm, Sat 9am–1pm.
The Archaeological Museum: Lomo 9.
Tel: (922) 371465. Open: Tue–Sat
10am–1pm & 6–9pm, Sun 10am–1pm.*

Bananera el Guanche
Despite its obvious mass tourist appeal,
the cultivation of this miniature banana
plantation is well explained, and its lush,
terraced gardens hold an extensive range
of indigenous and exotic plants. There is
an area of over 400 cacti, and a small
collection of farmyard animals.
*3km southeast of Puerto on La Orotava
Rd. Tel: (922) 331853. Open: daily
9am–6pm. Admission charge. Free bus
from Playa Martiánez.*

Jardín Botánico (Botanic Garden)
This is the oldest of Puerto's attractions,
founded in 1788 by King Carlos III as a
halfway house Jardín de Aclimatación
(Acclimatisation Garden) for plants
travelling from the tropics to Spain. It's

The Lido de Martiánez, 3.2 hectares of recreational abandonment

a small, shady place with over 200 species of plants and trees crowding into just 2.5 hectares. Most people's favourite is the giant 200-year-old South American fig tree in the centre, a menacing gothic mass of intertwined roots and branches.

If you prefer flowers to trees and shrubs, **La Rosaleda** rose gardens are nearby, with over 15,000 roses and waterplants, and many birds.

The exotic terraced gardens of Bananera el Guanche

Jardín Botánico: 2km southeast of centre, Calle Retama on La Orotava Rd. Tel: (922) 384751/378035. Fax: (922) 384751. Open: daily 9am–6pm. Admission charge. La Rosaleda: 3km southeast of centre, Calle Camino Lazo. Open: daily 9am–5pm. Admission charge. Free bus from Playa Martiánez.

Lido/Lago Martiánez (Lido/Pool Martiánez)

Until the opening of Puerto's Playa Jardín, the Lido Martiánez was the town's unofficial 'beach'. It was designed by César Manrique (*see pp68–9*) in 1969, and brilliantly solved the problem of Puerto's beachless seafront. This beautifully laid out series of pools and fountains, palm-shaded sunbathing terraces, and black and white lava rockery covers three hectares.

Playa Martiánez. Tel: (922) 383852. Open: daily 9am–6pm. Admission charge.

Loro Parque (Parrot Park)

This Florida-style wildlife park maintains very high standards of both conservation and entertainment. Set in superb tropical gardens, it was conceived as a parrot park, and is said to contain the world's largest collection of parrots. It has also recently added the largest dolphinarium outside America, a huge aquarium with sharks which claims the largest underwater tunnel in the world, a gorilla jungle, and a bat cave. Other attractions include a 180-degree special effects cinema, parrot shows, and performing sealions. There are crocodiles, tigers, and the biggest penguinarium in the world.

Calle San Felipe, 3km west in Punta Brava district. Tel: (922) 374081. Fax: (922) 375021. www.loroparque.com Open: daily 8.30am–5pm. Admission charge. Bus: free from Playa Martiánez & Playa de las Américas every 20 minutes.

Playa Jardín

This new black-sand beach was opened in 1992–3. The crashing Atlantic waves have been tamed by a man-made reef comprising some 4,000 20-tonne concrete blocks (submerged out of sight), and the back of the beach area was landscaped under the direction of César Manrique. Adjacent is the 17th-century Castillo de San Felipe, which has been re-opened as a cultural centre.

Open: Mon–Fri 10am–1pm, 6–9pm.

Santa Cruz

Santa Cruz is the capital of Tenerife and the administrative centre of the western islands. It is also an important port. To most holiday visitors, however, it means a morning's 'tax-free' shopping in the Calle del Castillo, and a visit to the town's most colourful bazaar, the Mercado de Nuestra Señora de África.

A dazzling palette of blue seas around Santa Cruz

Santa Cruz is more than just a place to shop; it's a busy, though rarely stressful, typical Canarian town with a grand, somewhat faded air.
Santa Cruz is 36km northeast of Puerto de la Cruz. Tourist office: Cabildo Insular, Plaza de España. Tel: (922) 605500.
Open: Mon–Fri 8am–6pm,
Sat 9am–1pm.

Iglesia de Nuestra Señora de la Concepción (Church of Our Lady of the Conception)

This early 16th-century church is Santa Cruz's most important historical building, currently under restoration.
Plaza de la Iglesia.

Mercado de Nuestra Señora de África (Market of Our Lady of Africa)

This colourful, bustling market sells a wide range of fruits, vegetables, flowers, fish, and meats. On Sundays, a *rastro* (flea-market) is held next to the halls.
Across Puerte Serrador.
Open: Mon–Sat 9am–1pm.

Museo de la Naturaleza y el Hombre (Museum of Man and Nature)

Located in the old Civil Hospital, the centre houses the former Archaeological Museum and the Museum of Natural Sciences. Themes include 'The Canary Islands Through Time', and 'Biological Anthropology'.
Calle Fuente Morales. Tel: (922) 213422.
Open: Tue–Sun 10am–5pm.
Admission charge.

Museo Municipal de Bellas Artes (Municipal Museum of Fine Arts)

The pride of this museum is its fine collection of works by Flemish and Spanish masters, including Ribera, Brueghel, Van Loo, and Jordaens.
Calle José Murphy. Tel: (922) 244358.
Open: Mon–Fri 10am–1.30pm, 2.30–7pm (winter), 10am–7.30pm (summer).
Free admission.

Parque Municipal García Sanabria

This is a beautifully laid out park with exotic trees and shrubs, fountains and statuary, a floral clock, and a small animal compound.

En route to the park are two plazas – Plaza del General Weyler, and Plaza 25 de Julio with ceramic benches decorated with museum-piece 1920s tiles.
Rambla del General Franco–Calle Mendez Nuñez.

Plaza de España

The drab, towering cross which stands in this square is a monument to the dead of the Spanish Civil War (1936–9). Next to it is another depressing example of Fascist architecture, the huge *Cabildo Insular* (island government offices).

Plaza de la Candelaria

The centre of this square is dominated by a statue illustrating El Triunfo de la Candelaria (Triumph of the Virgin of Candelaria, *see p100*) by the renowned Italian sculptor Antonio Canova (1757–1822). The figures on guard at the corner represent Guanche chieftains (*see pp14–15*).

Look into the bank at No. 9 on the Plaza. This was formerly the Palacio de Carta, built in 1742, and contains a perfect example of a Canarian patio. Calle del Castillo, leading off from here, is the town's main shopping street.

Santa Cruz de Tenerife

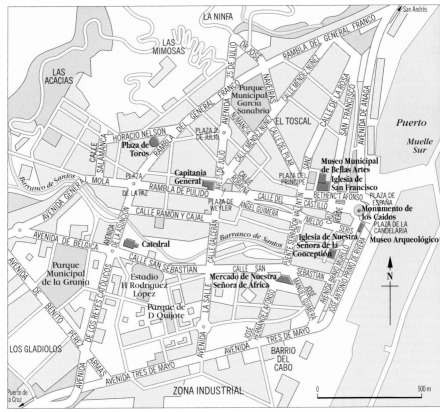

Southern Resorts

The once separate resorts of Los Cristianos and Playa de las Américas have now all but joined to become the second largest resort in the Canary Islands (after Maspalomas on Gran Canaria), and one of the biggest in all Spain. The reason for their success is based on two factors: all-year-round sunshine, and an ability to cater for hundreds of thousands of package holidaymakers a year.

Barranco del Infierno

Despite its fearsome name ('Hell's Gorge'), this lush ravine is the only place where you will find natural running water in the harsh and arid landscape of southern Tenerife. A popular walk along the ravine is signposted, and takes around 2½ hours there and back.
6km north of Playa de las Américas.

El Abrigo

There are few places in the south where good local restaurants may easily be found, and picturesque fishing villages are even scarcer. El Abrigo is such a place to sample the local fish delicacies.
15km east of Los Cristianos.

El Médano

This small, developing resort has the best of the southern beaches, but with gusts that often sandblast its occupants.
22km east of Los Cristianos.

La Caleta

One of the best places of the island to sample the local fish. It has a pleasant beach as well.
10km north of Playa de las Américas.

Los Cristianos

One of the most popular resorts in the Canary Islands, Los Cristianos draws a slightly older clientele than Playa de las Américas, and has two advantages over its neighbour. First, if you look hard among the new developments you can still find vestiges of the old settlement. Second, its harbour provides a changing mix of fishing boats, pleasure craft and ferries chugging to and from La Gomera. There is

THE EAST

Two contrasting points of interest are located in the region.

The Basilica of Candelaria (17km south of Santa Cruz) holds a statue of Nuestra Señora de la Candelaria, the patron saint of all the Canary Islands. On the Plaza de la Candelaria there are statues of Guanche chieftains, who once worshipped the same Virgin.

The Ethnographic Park (25km south of Santa Cruz) has the stepped Pirámides de Guímar, which have conflicting theories on their origin and age.

a small, sandy beach which looks on to the harbour. Nearby are: **Cactus and Animal Park**; **Jardines del Atlantico Bananera**, a guided tour around a banana plantation; there is also a theme park **Amazonia**, a large tropical garden with free-flying butterflies and humming birds; **Tenerife Zoo**, **Monkey Park**, and **Eagles Park** are also here.

Los Cristianos is 15km west of Reina Sofia airport. Cactus and Animal Park is on the Las Galletas road, between Los Cristianos and Guaza (tel: (922) 795424). Jardines del Atlantico Bananera, Buzanada, is between Las Galletas and Valle de San Lorenzo (tel: (922) 720961). Amazonia is near exit 26 Autopista Sur (tel: (922) 795424). Tenerife Zoo and Monkey Park, Llano Azul (tel: (922) 795424/790720). Eagles Park is 3km from Los Cristianos, off the road to Arona (tel: (922) 753001). All these sites are open daily 10am–6pm. There is a free bus from Los Cristianos or Playa de las Américas.

Playa de las Américas

The boom-town resort of Playa de las Américas was built in the late 1960s as a home-from-home for north European package holidaymakers. There is little that is Canarian, and unless you are happy drinking pints of British beer and eating food 'just like Mother makes', then this place probably isn't for you. Beaches are dark sand. Many tourists decamp to **Aguapark Octopus** (waterpark), at San Eugenio.

17km west of Reina Sofia airport. Tourist Office: Pueblo Canario. Tel: (922) 793390. Open: Mon–Fri 9am–3.30pm. Aguapark Octopus: San Eugenio, 2km east of the centre. Tel: (922) 715266/ 714270. Open: daily 10am–6pm. Admission charge.

Playa Paraiso

This is a new, and as yet still quiet resort. The dark, sandy beaches are great for sunbathing.

Dining al fresco on Playa de las Américas

Drive: Anaga Peninsula

This excursion takes in the highlights of the northeast peninsula, from the green peaks of the Anaga mountains to the golden sands of Playa de las Teresitas. Choose a clear day to get the best from the *miradores* (viewpoints) en route. (This drive may also be combined with the walk on pages 106–7.)

Aim to arrive at the Casa de Carta museum as it opens at 10am (closed Friday), then allow around 3 hours, excluding stops, to reach Las Teresitas beach.

Start from Tacoronte.

1 Tacoronte

This straggling town, 20km east of Puerto de la Cruz, is famous for its wine, and two fine churches: the 17th-century Iglesia de Santa Catalina, and, close by, the Iglesia del Cristo de los Dolores, which holds a much revered 17th-century statue of Christ.

Take the TF122 north, noting the ancient dragon tree as you are leaving town.

2 Casa de Carta (near Valle Guerra)

An excellent ethnographic museum in an 18th-century house (*see p84*).
Open: 10am–1pm & 3–6pm (summer), 4–7pm (winter).

Continue on the TF122 for 4km, turn right at Tejina onto the TF121 and continue for 12km through Tegueste, Las Canteras, and Las Mercedes, stopping to admire the Miradores de Jardina and Cruz del Carmen. After another 1½km, turn left (signposted towards Las

Carboneras). Continue straight ahead, past the second Carboneras sign, to Taborno (13km past Cruz del Carmen).

3 Taborno

This small village is situated high among the Anaga peaks at 1,024m, and consequently enjoys marvellous views.
Retrace your route to where you turned left towards Las Carboneras. Carry straight on, then rejoin the main TF123 road. This scenic road continues for 8km along the top of the cumbre *(ridge), with views to north and south offering a glimpse of the golden sands of Las Teresitas. Turn off left towards El Bailadero.*

4 El Bailadero

A spectacular *mirador* (*see p85*), at which point you can either turn round and go south (left) to Las Teresitas beach and Santa Cruz, go south and then turn north to Taganana (*see p85*), or continue east (straight ahead) for 6km to Chamucadas, where there is another fine *mirador*. Shortly after, the road ends.

From El Bailadero head south on the TF112 to San Andrés.

5 Playa de las Teresitas

It is estimated that this golden strip, brought over from the Sahara, constitutes some 4 million sackfuls of sand. It is a superb beach with safe, shallow waters and mountain backdrops; well maintained, it is rarely very busy, and is unspoilt by surrounding developments. The adjacent village of San Andrés is renowned for its fish restaurants. Notice its ruined castle, neatly smashed in half by a flood tide some 30 years ago. *Continue back along the coastal road for 8km to the waterfront of Santa Cruz.*

6 Santa Cruz

Just before you reach the centre of town, look for the Club Náutico (Yacht Club), beside which are the remains of the

The densely forested Anaga Mountains around Taborno

Castillo de Paso Alto. From here Santa Cruz enjoyed its finest military moment in 1797, repulsing an attack by Admiral Lord Nelson and shooting off the lower part of his right arm, to boot.

It's often surprisingly easy to park close to the centre of town on the main road, if you arrive by early evening. The streets come alive again after siesta – a good time to visit the capital.

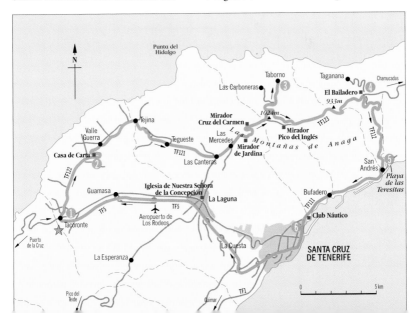

Walk: Puerto de la Cruz

Puerto de la Cruz remains at heart a Spanish colonial town with many tangible reminders of its past. This walk will show you a little of the town's history and architecture. Avoid Monday if you wish to visit the Archaeological Museum.

Allow 1–1½ hours (excluding time spent in the Museum).

Start from the El Peñon (the Rock) religious monument, next to the football stadium.

1 Calle de San Felipe

This is a charming old street of one-storey fishermen's houses, and some good local restaurants. Look out for the unusual green decorated oriel window at No. 16.

Turn left into Calle de Pérez Zamora, and left again into Calle de Lomo.

2 Calle de Lomo

The **Museo Arqueológico** (Archaeological Museum) is housed in a fine 19th-century mansion. It stages temporary exhibitions.

Retrace your steps to Calle de San Felipe.

3 Plaza del Charco

This handsome square marks the centre of town. Look into the Rincón del Puerto, a fine, typical Canarian balconied courtyard, built in 1739.

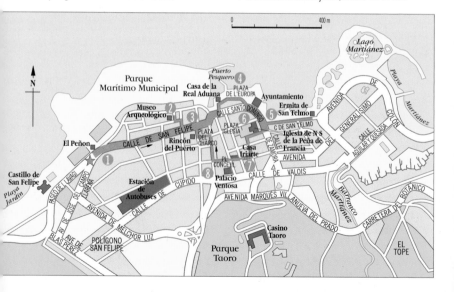

Continue on Calle de San Felipe and turn left.

4 Puerto Pesquero (Fishing Port)
To the right-hand side of the port, the beautiful black and white stone house is the **Casa de la Real Aduana** (Royal Custom House), the oldest building in town, dating from 1620. Note the fortifications to the seaward side. On the opposite side of the street is the Casa Miranda, dating from around 1730.

A little further on is a new square with cannons, the Plaza de l'Europa, from which there are good sea views. To the right are the Casas Consistoriales (town hall offices, built in 1973).
Turn left on to Calle de San Telmo.

5 Calle de San Telmo
The start of this promenade is known as the **Punta del Viento** (Windy Point), marked by a modern sculpture of a windswept girl. Below, the waves break spectacularly into the black-lava rockpools. The tiny, snow-white Ermita de San Telmo (Church of St Elmo) dates from the 18th century.
Retrace your steps to the start of the promenade; continue on for a few yards then turn right into Calle La Hoya, which leads to Plaza Iglesia.

6 Plaza Iglesia
Note the old-fashioned *bodega* (wine-shop) on the left before entering the square. This is Puerto's loveliest plaza, with an elegant swan fountain in the centre. The Iglesia de Nuestra Señora de la Peña de Francia (Church of Our Lady of the Rock of France) is a beautiful 16th-century building with Baroque

Just strolling on Calle de San Telmo

altarpieces and side-chapels. The Hotel Marquesa (1712), and the Hotel Monopol (1742), also on the square, both possess typical balconied patios.
Leave the Plaza by Calle Cólogan and take the second street Calle Iriarte (right).

7 Casa Iriarte
An 18th-century house with a balcony onto the street, and a lovely interior patio. It houses craft-sellers (mostly embroidery), and a small naval museum.

8 Palacio Ventosa
On the pretty square diagonally opposite the Casa Iriarte is the Colegio San Agustín. This occupies the 18th-century Palacio Ventosa, of which the most notable feature is the tall tower.
Turn right into Calle Blanco. This leads back to the Plaza del Charco.

Museo Arqueológico *Tel: (922) 209317.* Open: Tue–Sat 10am–1pm & 6–9pm, Sun 10am–1pm. Admission charge.
Casa Iriarte *Tel: (922) 383311.* Shop and museum open: Mon–Sat 9.30am–7pm. Admission charge to museum.
Palacio Ventosa Although not officially open to the public, it can be seen at close quarters from the college grounds during term time.

Walk: Chinamada

This walk takes you into the heart of the Anaga Mountains, to a village which, until 1993, was cut off from all roads, and where the inhabitants still live in caves carved into the mountainside. It's an easy walk to follow, and suitable for all ages. Much of the first half could be undertaken in a four-wheel drive vehicle or even an ordinary car, though the track is quite bumpy.

Allow 1½–2 hours.

Start from Las Carboneras (see map, p103, on how to get there).

1 Las Carboneras

This small village comprises two bars, a church, and a handful of houses.
Start by the main plaza and follow the wooden sign, posted to Chinamada (where the road proper finishes and the new track begins).

2 Roque de Taborno

The first stretch of the walk is dominated by the green, velvety peak of Roque de Taborno, away to your right. This rises to 706m and has a distinctive, bullet-like basalt peak. In winter the wonderful sweet smell of the *retama* plant fills the air along the route.
After about 15 minutes, the track turns around the corner away from Roque de Taborno, but still offers fine views. Hillside caves now begin to appear. Turn the next bend and the first cave houses of Chinamada are to the right-hand side of the track. Ignore these and follow the track, which wiggles to the left through a tiny pass and continues ahead.

3 Barranco del Tomadero

The view to the left of the track, across the deep green ravine that separates Chinamada from the tiny white houses of Batán, is stunning. This ravine runs all the way to the sea at Punta del Hidalgo. Goats graze on these seemingly impossibly steep, terraced slopes, providing meat and cheese for the people of Chinamada.

4 Chinamada

Note the fine dragon tree to the right of the path. A recently built chapel stands straight ahead of you. The houses of the 30 or so people who live here are small and cut back into the rocky ridge but, as you will see, they are hardly Stone Age. You can walk along the narrow path alongside the houses. If you are feeling inspired by the scenery, it's around an hour's walk all the way down to Punta del Hidalgo (from where buses run back to La Laguna).
Return the short distance to the small crossroads and climb the hill up the steps to the right, signposted Las Escaleras (The Stairs).

5 Las Escaleras

The steps don't last for long, descending down to a narrow path. This is a pretty route, strewn with ferns and Canary bell flowers. The path initially skirts the hillside. There's only one route to follow, and a metal conduit runs along the side of the path as a guide.

After about 30 minutes you will see the main road down to your left. At this point you can descend and walk back to the village (half a kilometre), or continue along the path for another 10–15 minutes to the Mirador de las Escaleras, which offers yet another fine aspect of these

The path running past Chinamada leads right down to the sea

majestic hills. Follow the path back and make the descent to the road.

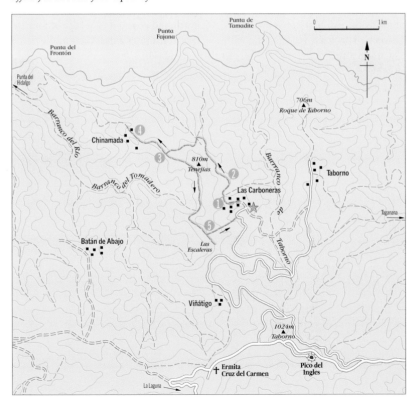

La Gomera

La Gomera is a dome-shaped island with a sunken central plateau, its sides rent by great gullies which almost completely segment it. This tortuous terrain once presented great communication problems and still adds to journey times. The island may be only 23 by 25km at its widest points, but you won't be able to drive round it comfortably in a day, and a minimum of two days is required to see all the island's highlights.

Leading the goats to pastures new

It would be a shame not to stay overnight on Gomera, since here are arguably the two best hotels in all the Canaries. This really is a case of quality against quantity as, aside from these two, there are only a few other small hotels and pensions. The lack of tourism here constitutes at least half of the

The scenic village of Agulo with Mount Teide in the distance

appeal to the island's small group of admirers, although with the ferry and flight connections to Tenerife, La Gomera is fast becoming a hiker's and nature-lover's paradise. The comparison between La Gomera and Los Cristianos, just 32km and 35 minutes away by hydrofoil, reveals two wholly different cultures.

With only one real beach on the whole island, and a limited tourism infrastructure, it seems unlikely that this will change much.

First impressions here are misleading. The barren landscape around San Sebastián soon gives way to some of the most beautiful, luxuriant valleys in the archipelago, while the centre of the island is almost permanently covered in mist, refreshing the thirsty prehistoric national park rainforest.

There are few sights as such on Gomera, but natural beauty is here in abundance. To get the best from the island, bring your walking boots and stay for a week.

La Gomera

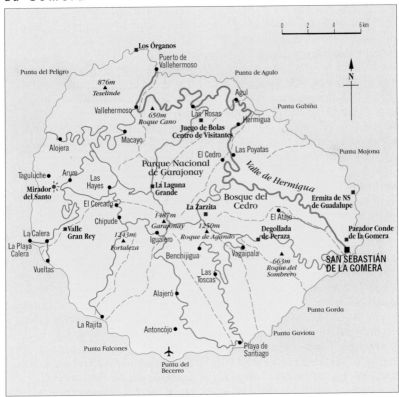

Northern La Gomera

The road to the north of La Gomera is a spectacular winding route calling at the island's most picturesque settlements. If you have just one day on the island, this is the way to go. It also has the advantage of being lower than the southern route, avoiding the clouds which form on the higher ground. Without these, however, there would be no primordial laurasilva forest on Gomera – a feature much enjoyed by walkers and naturalists.

The children's playground at Vallehermoso – ancient deities or modern art?

Agulo

The adjectives 'neat and tidy' perfectly describe this small, pretty village of narrow, cobbled streets. Its position is perfect – enclosed in a natural amphitheatre of rocky cliffs perched high above the sea, with Tenerife's Mount Teide forming a majestic backdrop. In the centre is a curiously designed grey and white painted church with Moorish-influenced domes.
25km northwest of San Sebastián.

Hermigua

Hermigua, the second largest settlement on the island after San Sebastián, is a long, straggling village clinging to the roadside above a lush valley of banana plantations. Vines are also grown here, strung on bamboo frames which hang diagonally across the hillsides like giant spiders' webs.

Visit the Los Telares craft centre (on the main road) to see the old house where girls still weave on ancient looms. A little further along, stop by the Convento sign. By the side of the plaza is the 16th-century Convento de Santo Domingo, with a fine ceiling and an image of the local saint.
Tourist office: Tel: (922) 144025. 20km northwest of San Sebastián.

Juego de Bolas Centro de Vistantes

This excellent visitor centre should be able to answer most questions you may have about La Gomera. Well-labelled gardens illustrate island flora, a small ethnographical museum covers peasant life, and a complex of workshops demonstrates basketry, weaving, pottery, and woodworking. In the main reception area are displays giving information about the Garajonay National Park.

The road between the visitor centre and the El Tabor bar leads to a newly created *mirador* with spectacular views right down on top of Agulo and across to Tenerife. The unsurfaced track at the end of the asphalt road may be very bumpy, but is quite short and manageable in an ordinary car.
The visitor centre is 34km northwest of San Sebastián. Tel: (922) 800993. Open: Tue–Sun 9.30am–4.30pm.

Parque Nacional de Garajonay (Garajonay National Park)

This 4,000-hectare national park, which is slightly more than 10 per cent of the total area of the island, occupies the island's central high plateau, and owes its protected status to its Canarian laurasilva forest – the largest and most complete known example of the ecosystem left in the world. Laurasilva (a woodland of ferns, laurels, and heath trees) thrives in damp conditions, and much of the forest is cloaked in a veil of mist year-round. In 1986, it was declared a World Heritage Site by UNESCO. During the winter, it is cold and damp, but in summer it dries to an extent where forest fires are a hazard. The trails within are popular with walkers. There are two information centres: at La Laguna Grande (*see p114*) and Juego de Bolas. The highest point on the island, El Alto de Garajonay (Mount Garajonay), at 1,487m, falls within the park, and on a good day offers excellent views.

Vallehermoso

This compact village hugging the valley side is a fine sight when approached from the TF112 to the north. At the entrance to Vallehermoso is a particularly artistic children's playground. The giant sculpture of three curvaceous ladies with headdresses would grace many a modern art museum. Vallehermoso has a lively centre with two bustling *tapas* bars, from which old houses rise up to the church.

Tourist office: Tel: (922) 800181.
42km northwest of San Sebastián.

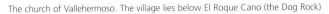

The church of Vallehermoso. The village lies below El Roque Cano (the Dog Rock)

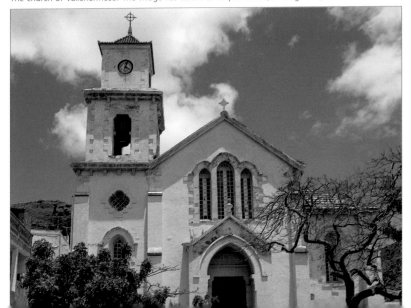

San Sebastián

Your first view of La Gomera, from the ferry, will be of the island capital, San Sebastián. If the fishing fleet is in, and if the long-term restorations to beach and harbour have been finished, you may well like it. San Sebastián is famous for its Columbus associations (he sailed from here in 1492), but makes light of it – there are few exhibits or memorabilia of this era.

The ferry terminal at San Sebastián harbour

Iglesia de la Asunción (Church of the Assumption)

This ancient church on Calle del Medio is the one site in San Sebastián that we know Columbus visited. Records tell us he prayed here in 1492, even though most of the present church dates from the 16th century. It's a fine building, with beautiful woodwork, notably the ceiling and the balcony above the entrance doors. Note, too, the mural depicting the town's defence against an English fleet in 1734.

A little further along Calle del Medio is the **Casa Colón/Casa Columbina**. The veracity of a Columbus connection is doubtful here, but occasionally the house stages Columbus exhibitions.

Parador Conde de la Gomera (Parador of the Count of Gomera)

Step into the beautiful *parador* courtyard, and peeping out from behind the luxuriant plants you'll see portraits of Columbus and other historical worthies. Here, more than anywhere in San Sebastián, the spirit of the age is conjured up. It comes as something of a disappointment to learn that this state hotel was built in 1973. It is a glorious

reproduction of a typical aristocratic island mansion, but has no historical pedigree whatsoever (*see p169*).
Lomo de la Horca (signposted from the harbour).

Pozo de Colón (Well of Columbus)

It is known that Columbus's men took water from La Gomera to the New World, and as the hole in the ground here is the nearest well to the harbour, logic has it that this must be 'the well that baptised America'. The well is only accessible through the old Casa del Pozo de la Aguada (House of the Well), formerly the Custom House, and now the Tourist Office.
*Calle Real 4. Tel: (922) 141512/140147;
fax: (922) 140151;
www.gomera-island.com
Open: 9am–1pm & 4–6pm (summer),
9am–1.30pm & 3.30–6pm (winter).*

Torre del Conde (Tower of the Count)

This sturdy pink and white brick tower was built in 1447 by the first Count of Gomera, Hernán Peraza the Elder. His namesake son became something of a tyrant and was killed by

Guanches at the Degollada de Peraza
(*see box*), reputedly after being lured to a
love nest nearby. His wife, Beatriz de
Bobadilla, was notorious throughout
Spanish royal circles for her promiscuity.
She is said to have entertained
Columbus in the tower and rumours
speak of an affair.

The tower was also used for storing
riches from the New World en route to
Spain. It is expected to open sometime
in the future as an exhibition area.
Next to the harbour front.

Los Roques
The main southern route from San Sebastián
(TF713) passes a number of outstanding
volcanic plug rock formations. Most
interesting is the **Roque del Sombrero**
(8km from town), which resembles a pointed
Chinese hat, peaking at 663m. After 16km
there is a spectacular, if windy *mirador* at the
Degollada (Pass) de Peraza. Looming above it
is the mightiest of the rocks, **Roque de
Agando** (1,250m). Three notable *roques* on
the other side of the road from east to west
are: **Carmen** (1,140m), **Zarcita** (1,235m),
and **Ojila** (1,169m).

San Sebastián, dwarfed by its surroundings

Southern La Gomera

The south of La Gomera accommodates the island's two tourist resorts, Playa de Santiago, and Valle Gran Rey. Yet both are relatively isolated, and would hardly even register on the average Canarian holiday development scale. The Valle Gran Rey was, until recently, only known by a few hippy-types, whereas the hotel complex at Playa de Santiago attracts a monied clientele. The effect of the new airport on these places is yet to be seen.

Primitive in style, the pottery at El Cercado is shaped by hand

El Cercado/Chipude

These neighbouring hamlets, divided by a ridge, could almost be twins. Chipude is the more handsome of the pair, enjoying a splendid setting against the foot of the table-top mountain known as La Fortaleza (1,243m). In El Cercado you can see the craft of *alfareria* – pottery made from the dark Gomeran earth, without a wheel.
El Cercado is 37km northwest of San Sebastián. Chipude is 39km northwest of San Sebastián.

La Laguna Grande

The 'big lagoon' has long gone, but this is a popular meeting point for walkers, as it is an entrance point to the Garajonay National Park (*see p111*). There is an information office and a log cabin, which in winter has a roaring fire. For non-walkers there is also a children's playground and a barbecue area.
29km northwest of San Sebastián. Open: Tue–Sat 9am–4.30pm. On Fri walking tours depart from here. Reservations are essential. Tel: (922) 800993 (Juego de Bolas office).

Playa de Santiago

The stony beach here is in the infancy of development, with a handful of bars and restaurants lining its new promenade. At the far end is a small fishing port. Above the beach, the Hotel Jardín Tecina is very much in the vanguard of Gomeran tourism. With over 400 rooms, this is a veritable giant, but it has not abused its power. The

LOS ORGANOS

Los Organos (the organ pipes) is an extraordinary 200m-wide formation of slender, tightly-packed basalt columns. Some of these reach over 80m high and they do, indeed, resemble giant petrified church organ pipes.

Los Organos is located just off the north coast and may only be viewed from the sea. Boats depart from Valle de Gran Rey, Playa de Santiago and San Sebastián. For further details contact the tourist information office in San Sebastián.

architecture is vernacular, and rooms are in village-style bungalows, set in beautifully laid out grounds. Excursions and walking tours may be organised here through the Gomera Safari travel agency. Notice the colourful statues outside the hotel. The grinning *conquistador* is understandably pleased with himself, but the native Indian (presumably meant to be a Guanche) looks as if he would be far more at home in North America.

34km southwest of San Sebastián. Tourist office: Tel: (922) 146000.

Valle Gran Rey

The origin of the name 'Valley of the Great King' goes back to Guanche times, but this is still a place fit for royalty.

There is only one road into the valley, and it is arguably the most beautiful on the island. Towards the bottom the views to the emerald green slopes on the far side are breathtaking, with row upon row of little white houses perched precariously on steep terraces.

At the valley bottom, the road splits – left to the port, right to **La Playa Calera**. The latter is the only sandy beach on the island, and is showing signs of small-scale development. The pretty village of La Calera lies behind the resort.

En route to the Valle Gran Rey, stop at the **Mirador del Santo** at Arure (10km north of La Calera). It is one of the finest viewpoints on the island.

Valle Gran Rey is 52km west of San Sebastián.

The precipitous slopes of Valle Gran Rey; the valley floor is rich in palms and bananas

Walk: Vallehermoso

This walk combines Gomeran landscapes of lush valleys in deep ravines, overlooked by volcanic rocks, with a charming reservoir. It is suitable for any age and fitness level, although the hill is reasonably steep, and much of it could be followed in an ordinary car.

Allow 1–1½ hours.

Start in the centre of Vallehermoso, and follow the road uphill out of town, to the left of the Bar Route Amaya.

1 Roque Cano

The large 'Canine Rock', which protrudes 650m into the sky and dominates the view, is named after its resemblance to a canine tooth. Like so many other volcanic outcrops on the island, it is merely the central volcanic lava plug – the rest of the cone has long been eroded away. As you continue to

Vallehermoso church, at the start of the walk

EL SILBO

Compelled by the difficulties imposed by the landscape, the Gomerans have developed a unique language known as *el silbo* (the whistle). This is no ordinary whistling; it has real modulation, vocabulary, and stentorian volume. It is said that some *silbadores* can communicate from up to 5km away. With the advent of tele-communications, and the decline of ancient skills, practitioners are becoming rare. The gardener at the *parador* may well demonstrate *silbo* for you; otherwise, join the tourist show at Las Rosas restaurant (*see p165*).

climb, look back for fine views of Vallehermoso and its church. Down to your left, the abundance of the lush valley is clear. Bananas, palm trees, sugar cane, orange groves, and vines all jostle for space.
Continue your climb up the hill, which becomes steeper and rounds a bend.

2 The Valley of 1001 Palms

It is doubtful whether anyone has really counted the trees here, but as many are on tap for Gomera's famous palm-honey (*see p163*), it is possible. Look for metal cups attached to the trunks, catching the 'honey' (palm sap). Metal bands on the trees keep the ants at bay.

Whatever the number of trees, this valley is a splendid sight, particularly in the late afternoon, as the sun shines directly down into it.
After about 20 minutes' walking, you will see the dam wall holding back the reservoir.

3 Embalse de la Encantadora

Despite its function, supplying water to the village and valleys below, this reservoir has a natural, almost ornamental look, hence its romantic name – the Lake of the Enchanted Lady. Ducks bob on its surface, and there is a statue of a man – perhaps a Guanche – stranded on a tiny island with just a pole for company. Walk all the way around the reservoir. You'll probably meet a goat or two en route, tethered and grazing. As you complete the circle, cross the metal bridge, and (if you don't suffer from vertigo) look down the sheer wall of the dam, trickling water into the valley.

Walk back down the hill and take the right turn downhill.

Down here is a very ramshackle smallholding of animals and birds. Don't mind the barking dog (as long as he is attached to his tether!). The path descends all the way to the foot of the dam where there is a small stream. You can cross this to the orange groves on the other side, but you can go no further.
Return to the main road and descend back down into the village.

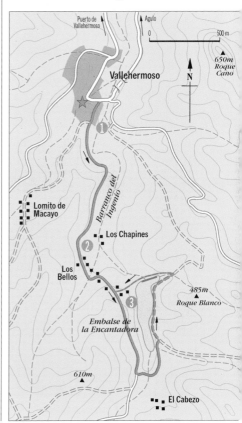

La Palma

La Palma is quite unlike the other, smaller Canary islands, and in many ways stands superior to its larger cousins. It is known throughout the Canaries as La Isla Verde (the Green Island), due to its comparative abundance of water. For the farmers this means profitable banana, tobacco, and avocado crops; for tourists it means the most tropical and, many would argue, the most beautiful landscape in the archipelago. This natural beauty is enhanced by the islanders' homes and gardens, often said to be the best kept in the Canaries.

Few tourists visit La Palma, although its natural beauty is unlike any other island in the Canaries

La Palma has a relatively prosperous history. Its capital, Santa Cruz de la Palma, was one of only three Spanish ports allowed to trade with the Americas for a period in the 16th century, and even today, its aristocratic past is visible.

The island doesn't excel in beach holidays. With just a few black beaches and its isolation from the major islands, it attracts only a handful of tourists in search of peace and natural beauty. Their main aim is the Caldera de Taburiente – a massive crater formed some 400,000 years ago by an earth-shattering explosion, subsequently smoothed and greened by nature into an outstanding beauty spot now enjoying Spanish national park status. By contrast, the most recent volcanic activity in the Canaries also happened on the island, in 1971. You can still feel the heat beneath your feet.

Two more features help explain the island's dramatic natural appeal. In relation to its surface area it lays claim to be the tallest island in the world. And if you reach the summit (at 2,426m), you will see a gleaming, white, astrophysical observation station, which would look right at home on the moon – for La Palma also boasts the clearest, darkest sky in the northern hemisphere.

Cultivating the slopes near Hoya Grande

La Palma

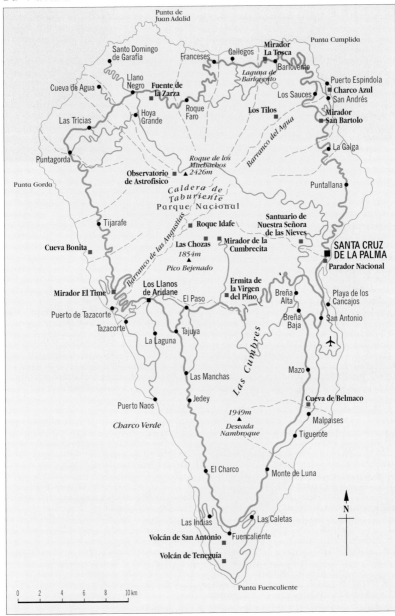

Northern La Palma

San Andrés aside, the northern villages of La Palma are unexceptional, and a tour of the whole northern loop can be a tiring experience. However, if the weather is clear, it is worth making the journey to the Roque de los Muchachos, which passes some of the island's most dramatic scenery, and ends in spectacular style, peering into the depths of Caldera de Taburiente.

Los Tilos

Los Tilos (the lime trees) is a damp ancient laurasilva forest of limes, laurels, myrtles, and ferns. Water flows so thick and fast here, down the Barranco del Agua, that a hydroelectric plant (the only one in the Canary Islands) has been constructed. There is a picnic area, and a visitor centre is planned.
29.5km north of Santa Cruz.

Parave Laguna de Barlovento

Just a few kilometres south of Barlovento, this lovely park has a charming lake with panoramic views of the countryside around.
*Tourism office:
Tel: (922) 696023.*

Puntagorda

This sparsely inhabited, straggling agricultural settlement lacks any real centre. However, the flower and vegetable fields around here are pretty, particularly in spring, when the pink almond trees bloom.
28km north of Los Llanos de Aridane.

Roque de los Muchachos

At 2,426m, this is the highest point on the island, perched on the edge of the Caldera de Taburiente (*see pp126–7*).

The road which leads here is tortuous, scenic (lunar-like in places), and passes through clouds before bursting back into sunlight near the top. This peak is always cold, and in winter is often covered in snow (in very bad weather the road is cut off). Having braved the journey, there are wonderful views down into

NORTHERN MIRADORES

There are two fine *miradores* to look out for while touring the north. Just north of La Galga (19km north of Santa Cruz), look for the signpost Mirador La Montaña. Stop by the small church of Ermita de San Bartolomé for a view along the east coast, then drive uphill to the Mirador San Bartolo, which has panoramic views inland.

At the very top of the island, just west of Barlovento, turn right towards Gallegos. After just over 1km the Mirador La Tosca gives views along the north coast. Look down to your right to a curious colony of dragon trees (*see p92*).

the *caldera* (crater), and nearby are the intriguing white domes of the Observatorio de Astrofísico (Astrophysical Observatory), which opened in 1985 (*see pp122–3*).
44km northwest of Santa Cruz.

San Andrés y los Sauces

The top half of this twinned village, Los Sauces, is a modern agricultural centre of little interest.

Take the road down through the dense banana plantations to San Andrés, where you will find a charming square shared by a 17th-century church, well-tended gardens, and a popular fish restaurant. From here old houses tumble down the steep cobbled hill towards the sea.

Near San Andrés is **Charco Azul** ('the Blue Pool'), a pleasantly situated semi-natural lido with refreshments.
San Andrés is 28km north of Santa Cruz.

Santuario de Nuestra Señora de las Nieves (Sanctuary of Our Lady of the Snows)

This is the most sacred spot on the island, though curiously 'the snows' refer not to the island peaks, but to a 4th-century miracle, when the Virgin appeared during an unusual snowfall in August in Rome.

The focus of attention is the 14th-century terracotta figure of the Virgin, the island's patron saint, and probably the oldest image in all the islands. There is some fine gold- and silver-work in the 17th-century chapel which houses the figure, and a restaurant in the square. Every five years (in August) the figure is brought down to Santa Cruz in a grand procession known as La Bajada de la Virgen (the descent of the Virgin). Great festivities follow. The next *bajada* is in the year 2005.
3½km west of Santa Cruz.

The Astrophysical Observatory at the highest point of the island

La Palma Observatory

Why on earth is the most important space observatory in the northern hemisphere sited on an obscure Canary Island? The answer is that La Palma provides a combination of geographical, topographical, and meteorological factors which are perfect for star-gazing.

The remoteness of the island and its lack of development means that the observatory (El Observatorio del Roque de los Muchachos) is free from distracting artificial light; the shape of the mountain and the prevailing winds mean the airflow here is comparatively undisturbed; and the site is above the clouds (which trap dust and moisture) for the vast majority of the year. Put all these together, and it means that extremely faint stars and galaxies, mind-boggling distances away, can be observed with the utmost clarity.

The observatory complex was inaugurated in 1985, and is host to a number of different international organisations. The largest observatory is operated by the English Royal Greenwich Observatory and includes the William Herschel telescope. This is the third largest in the world, but has the advantage of its La Palma site and the quality of its instrumentation over its two larger rivals, and is therefore probably the finest window on the universe in the world.

If you would like to see inside, the observatory is open only three times a

year, in summer (*tel: (922) 405500*). Don't expect to look through a working telescope, however. 'telescope time' here is fought over by professional astronomers from all over the world, and is usually three times over-subscribed.

Disappointingly for romantics, the popular image of the astronomer with his eye to the lens, wrapped in scarves to keep warm, is well out of date. Eyes are rarely put to lenses at La Palma, and the telescopes are remote-controlled from computer consoles, while operators sit in warm, comfortable rooms.

The William Herschel telescope and the campus where it is housed, reaching out to touch the clouds

Santa Cruz

Architecturally, Santa Cruz is one of the most handsome small towns in the archipelago. Its wealth from trade with the Americas may have passed, but its well-preserved buildings reflect a sense of prosperity. Tourism has hardly touched the town. There are two low-key museums here, and a *parador*, though you could walk past the latter and not even know it existed. But the town has plenty to offer in terms of authentic Spanish colonial atmosphere, and by night, the Avenida Marítima becomes a lively promenade of pavement bars and cafés.

Canarian houses on Avenida Marítima, decorated with Spanish colonial-style balconies

Avenida Marítima

Santa Cruz has one of the least spoiled seafronts of any town in the Canaries. At its southern end is a bizarre dragon tree with four 'heads' peering out on long 'necks', set at 90 degrees to the main trunk. The *parador* (*see p169*) is an appetiser for the splendid, balconied houses further along.

A little further along is the Castillo de Santa Catalina, built in the 16th century, though much altered in later years. Its entrance is to the rear, but it is presently closed to the public.

For hiking, touring and camping information, ask at the Tourism information office, Cabido Insular Ave. Maritm 3. Tel: (922) 411957.

Calle O'Daly

Running parallel to the Avenida Marítima, the cobbled Calle O'Daly reflects the 17th- and 18th-century wealth of the town, boasting several handsome merchants' houses. The street is named after an Irish banana merchant who settled on the island (towards the northern end it changes name to Calle Real). Walking from south to north, look out for Nos. 42, 38, 28, 26 and 24. Of special note is No. 22, built in the first half of the 17th century as the Palacio Salazar, and now housing the tourist office. After passing through the Plaza de España, visit the casino at No. 7 (or 15, depending on which numbering you follow). This building, a mix of Moorish and Colonial architecture, is now a social club. Just below is the delightful small square of Placeta de Borreo.

At the very end of the street is the surprising sight of a full-size galleon. It is a replica of Columbus's flagship, the *Santa María*, made of concrete. Columbus never actually called here, but the island did become wealthy on American trade, and this is also a monument to the town's 19th-century shipbuilders. Within it is a small **naval museum**.

Tourist information office: Calle O'Daly. Tel: (922) 412106.

Open: Mon– Fri 9am–1pm & 5–7pm, Sat 10.30am–1pm. Santa María naval museum open: Mon–Fri 9am–1pm & 5–7pm, Sat 10.30am–1pm. Admission charge.

Museo Insular (Island Museum)

The island's historical and ethnographical collection is housed in the 16th-century convent of San Francisco, which is located within the grounds of the church of the same name. This has been closed for some time, undergoing long-term restoration. *Calle San Francisco, off Calle O'Daly.*

Plaza de España

This fine ensemble of historic buildings is the heart of the capital. Look inside the 16th-century **Iglesia del Salvador** (Church of the Saviour).The ceiling is a splendid example of *mudéjar* (*see p153*) woodwork, and its Gothic arched sacristy is also notable. Its treasures include a painted altarpiece, and a remarkable silver cross in a rear chapel. Adjacent to the church is a fine drinking fountain. The beautiful building on the corner of the plaza now houses the well-known Spanish Open University.

The *ayuntamiento* (town hall) was built in 1569 with a Renaissance arcade and a fine colonial interior; it was once the Cardinal's palace. Step inside during office hours to admire the colourful mural by Mariano de Cossío on the stairway, and the outstanding carved panelling ceiling.
Iglesia del Salvador. Open: daily 8.30am–1pm & 4–8.30pm.

Plaza de España, the jewel in the crown of Santa Cruz

Southern La Palma

This southern loop of La Palma includes the most picturesque villages and, from Fuencaliente to Los Llanos de Aridane, the most scenic driving stretch of the island. Pine forests sweep down the hillside to pretty roadside hamlets, while superb coastal views open out ahead. The mountains loom ever closer and the Mirador de la Cumbrecita, the climax of the drive, provides unforgettable views into the Caldera de Taburiente.

Banana plantations below Tazacorte

Fuencaliente

This neat village is famous for its two volcanoes and its wine, both of which can easily be sampled by taking a walk around the volcanoes (*see pp128–9*), then visiting the *bodegas* (wine cellars). *33km south of Santa Cruz. Bodegas de Teneguía: Tel: (922) 447078. Open: Mon–Fri 9am–2pm & 3–5pm (winter), 8am–1pm (summer).*

Los Llanos de Aridane

It's easy to drive along the dual carriageway that bypasses Los Llanos and completely miss the old centre of town. Instead, turn right here (heading from Santa Cruz), and you will find a charming plaza with an early 16th-century church, Iglesia de los Remedios, a typically Canarian *ayuntamiento* (town hall), and café tables and chairs spreading beneath ancient Indian laurel trees. Step behind the church, and there are more fine old houses, and a view of the mountains. Nearby, the **Mirador El Time** offers spectacular views back along the south coast from an almost sheer elevation of 594m.

Los Llanos de Aridane is 32km west of Santa Cruz. Mirador El Time: Tel: (922) 489082/83.

Mazo

Saturday afternoon and Sunday morning markets bring tourists and locals to this small village. Do look into the fine 16th-century Iglesia de San Blás which has a number of 16th-century statues, and a fine high altar. Just outside the village on the road to Hoya de Maza is the highly regarded pottery workshop of El Molino (*see p145*).

Some 4km south of Mazo, Guanche inscriptions may be found in the Cueva (Cave) de Belmaco.
Mazo is 15km south of Santa Cruz.

Parque Nacional de la Caldera de Taburiente (National Park of the Crater of Taburiente)

The *caldera*, or crater, which comprises this protected area, measures 9km across at its widest point and has a circumference of 28km. It was formed some 400,000 years ago in a massive explosion, and since then the elements have gouged the crater even deeper (down to 900m), and have turned it into one of the most green and beautiful places in the archipelago.

There is only one surfaced road into the national park, and that is from the south, leading to the spectacular **Mirador de la Cumbrecita**. There is an information kiosk here, from where free guided walks start (pre-booking essential). There are more views from Lomo de Las Chozas, 1km due west. Serious walkers also enter the park from its southwest corner via the Barranco de las Angustias. This *barranco* (ravine) was the last bastion of La Palma's Guanches, and the great monolith known as **Roque Idafe** was a sacred point to them. *Mirador de la Cumbrecita is 30km west of Santa Cruz on Carretera General. Tel: (922) 497277.*

Tazacorte

The upper part of Tazacorte retains much of its old character, and is pleasantly laid out, with a promenade looking over dense green banana plantations down towards Puerto de Tazacorte. The focal point is a raised plaza where the locals sit under a bougainvillea-decked pergola next to a pretty church.

The fishing port of Puerto de Tazacorte, 3km to the north, has a black sand beach served by a handful of bars and restaurants.

The west coast's largest resort is Puerto Naos, 11km south of Tazacorte. This has a much larger beach, and on it the 300-bed, 4-star Sol Palma hotel – by far the biggest and most luxurious accommodation on the island. *Tazacorte is 38km west of Santa Cruz.*

The humbling power of Mother Nature; peering into Caldera de Taburiente, one of the world's deepest craters

Walk: La Palma Volcanoes

This walk shows you two of La Palma's volcanoes (one still warm!) in a spectacular coastal setting. The walk around Volcán de San Antonio is a level 30-minute circle open to everyone, although it does become slightly vertiginous on the far side. The walk down to Teneguía is rather steep, but you have the option of driving down to it. The walk up to the rim of Volcán de Teneguía is short but strenuous, and should not be attempted in windy weather.

Allow 1½–2 hours' total walking time if you descend all the way from Fuencaliente to Volcán de Teneguía – arrange (in the Bar Parada) for a taxi to collect you at the bottom.

To get to the Volcán de San Antonio, look out for the small sign on the main road in the middle of Fuencaliente opposite the Bar Parada. It's a 10-minute walk or a 2-minute drive to the crater car park. Follow the directional arrow that leads you anti-clockwise around the rim of the volcano.

The rim of the 300-year-old Volcán de San Antonio

1 Volcán de San Antonio

This 657-m high volcano erupted over the course of 66 days in 1667 and is now starting to look mature, with pine trees on its lower inner slopes and foliage higher up.

To your right, sloping down towards the sea, is the village of Las Indias. As you round the edge of the volcano there are excellent views back to the village of Fuencaliente (*see p126*), framed by evergreen hills. The volcano drops away steeply to the sea, and below are

wonderful views of Volcán de Teneguía. On a sunny day the volcano reveals its shades of browns, reds, and purples, but even when plain matt-black, it's a colourful sight against the clear blue Atlantic Ocean.

If you visit in summer, the space between the two volcanoes is covered in leafy vines, bright lime-green against the black lava-fields. The farmers of Fuencaliente have taken advantage of the natural disaster to cultivate some of the most unusual vines which thrive on this soil.

Just before you complete the circle around the rim, a path drops away to your right. Follow this, then follow the winding paths that snake downhill to Teneguía, which is clearly visible. Head for the car park.

Alternatively, if you want a shorter walk, return to your car, continue driving downhill, and take the sharp left turn towards Los Quemados. Take the track signposted 'Teneguía 1971', then take the first turning right, which takes you down to the car park. The ascent to the rim of the volcano takes 20–30 minutes.

2 Volcán de Teneguía

This is the youngest volcano in the archipelago, having erupted for 25 days as recently as 1971. It's said that the fountain of lava cascaded 200m into the air, and it produced the equivalent of two million lorry-loads of lava, but no one was hurt. Lava-streams spread down to the coast, towards the lighthouse and saltpans, and have actually extended the island by a few metres. Hot gases still emanate through the crater walls, and the ground is warm. Don't worry: the volcano is receding.

El Hierro

El Hierro is the most westerly, the smallest, and the least known of all the Canary Islands. As if to underline the point, Las Puntas (*see p133*) is the home of what is claimed to be the world's smallest hotel. Such solitude and lack of pretensions inevitably draw a small following of visitors who come here for the walking, and peace and quiet which is offered by the island.

The harbour at La Restinga

Surrounded by a rugged volcanic landscape, Candelaria Church at Frontera overlooks the sea

El Hierro

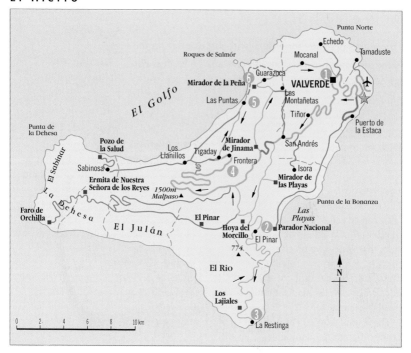

The history of the island is also fairly uneventful. The Herreños were the only Canarians to surrender peaceably to the Spanish invaders. Unfortunately, they did not foresee that the *conquistadores* would then sell them into slavery. According to popular belief, in 1493, Columbus may have called here during his second voyage to the New World; since then, not a lot has happened.

The great natural feature of El Hierro is the bay of **El Golfo** (the Gulf). This is thought to be the rim of a massive crater, half of which is submerged, and half of which rises dramatically to over 1,000m. El Hierro has other natural scenery to rival the best in the Canaries: splendid pine forests; strange, twisted juniper trees unique to the island; sheer mountain walls; and spectacular *miradores*.

There is, however, a shortage of accommodation. The *parador* would seem the most comfortable choice, but it is isolated, even by El Hierro standards. If you intend staying overnight, book ahead (*see p169*).

Touring can be frustrating. El Hierro may only be 24km by 27km at its maximum dimensions, but the configuration of its roads means that a good deal of backtracking is inevitable. The west of the island can only be explored along slow and bumpy dirt tracks, and the south coast is all but inaccessible.

Drive: El Hierro

This tour is designed for visitors with just one day on the island, and takes in virtually all the island highlights. For the route, see the El Hierro map on page 131.

Allow 5–6 hours.

From the airport follow the winding road inland for 7km.

1 Valverde

The island capital's only sign of importance is the sturdy late-18th-century church, Iglesia de la Concepción, that once gave protection against corsairs. Aside from a small ornamental plaza and a tourist office, it is essentially just a village. Surprisingly, there are two small museums here.

The **Exposición de Fondos Etnográficos y Arqueológicos** is above the tourist office, and exhibits old domestic implements and tools, and local folk costume; the **Museo Juan Padrón** is a private house with a collection of local antiquities at Calle Previsor Magdalena 8.

Head south through San Andrés and turn left towards El Pinar.

2 El Pinar

Gently rolling countryside of beautiful pine forests makes up this area with the small settlement of the same name at its heart.

Stop at the Mirador de las Playas for a wonderful view of the bay of Las Playas. The building with the red-tiled roof is the island *parador*.

Continue south for 13km.

3 La Restinga

This fishing port is marked by an ugly seawall which does at least create calm swimming conditions. Adventurous German tourists are cultivating La Restinga into something of a frontier resort. As you head along this road, note the strange rope-lava landscape just north of La Restinga.

Return to El Pinar and turn off left onto the secondary road towards Frontera. Turn left again as the road rejoins the main one.

4 Frontera

As the road descends to the coast, fine views of El Golfo appear. Tantalising views also appear of the church of Frontera (*see p130*). From afar it seems tiny and hopelessly isolated against the great green-grey mountain wall that makes up one side of El Golfo. But on closer inspection, this is just a small belltower built on a volcanic cone – the church itself is on the road below. Frontera is the island's wine-growing centre, and interested tourists may like to visit the large, deserted antique *lagares* (wine-presses) occasionally seen on the hillsides.

Continue on the TF912 to Tigaday; turn right to head downhill towards the sea.

5 Las Puntas

Aside from the 'world's smallest hotel' by the remains of the old harbour, there's not much at Las Puntas, but it's a pleasant drive down to the sea with its rocky outcrops. Almost directly above to the right is the Mirador de la Peña. *Backtrack all the way beyond Frontera, and after 20km turn left onto a minor road to the Mirador de Jinama. Continue, and turn left onto the main road.*

6 Mirador de la Peña

This superb, enclosed viewing point is the work of César Manrique (*see pp68–9*). The cliff on which it is perched falls almost a sheer 600m to the sea, offering the best view of El Golfo on the island. Note the strange native *sabina* (juniper) tree outside the *mirador*, grotesquely twisted by the fierce winds, yet still alive. A small forest of these exists at **El Sabinar** in the west of the island. *Return 8km east to Valverde and turn left to the airport.*

Tourist information office: Calle del Licenciado Bueno 1. *Tel: (922) 550302.* Open: Mon–Sat 8.30am–2.30pm. **Valverde museums** Both have unpredictable opening times; enquire at the tourist information office.

El Golfo from Mirador de Jinama. The village lies on the rim of half a volcanic crater, the other half of which is submerged beneath the sea

All distant isles attract myths and legends, and the hoariest island legend of all – Atlantis – is often connected with the Canaries. Plato described Atlantis as lying to the west of Gibraltar. Some 10,000 years before his time, so he wrote, it had been sent to the bottom of the ocean by earthquakes and tidal waves, until only seven mountain tops remained above the waters. Could this be the Canaries? Atlantis, a happy and wealthy land, also sounds rather like the Fortunate Islands, as the Canaries were described in antiquity – a land of plenty, of eternal springtime, with 'fertile soil and crops and fruit without working'.

Unfortunately for the romantics, this story does not match current theories suggesting that volcanoes created rather than destroyed the land. Plato's timescale was also inaccurate, as even the youngest islands are some two million years old.

And what should we make of the 'eighth Canary Island' – San Borondón? The island was named after St Brendan (or Brandan), a 6th-century Irish monk who sailed for seven years in search of the island where the saints were reincarnated. According to 16th-century Portuguese navigators, San Borondón lay 200–300 sea miles northwest of La Palma. By Canarian standards it was huge; 422km from north to south, and 149km from east to west. This island also had seven cities.

The legend continues that after seven years on the island, Brendan and his monks were told to leave by an angel. After yet another seven years, just as he was despairing of sighting land, an island (perhaps the same island) appeared. But immediately after the

Insulæ Forlu...

monks had celebrated mass, the land rumbled; they beat a hasty retreat back to their boat, and the island sank.

Apparently, when the weather conditions are right, you can look out northwest from La Palma, and see the high mountain peaks of San Borondón – but don't book your next holiday there just yet!

Picturesque maps illustrating the coming of Christianity to the archipelago date back to the 6th century. Evidence indicates that the islands were known to the ancient Greeks and Romans who called them Happy Islands, Garden of the Hesperides, Atlantida

Beyond the Resorts

Getting away from it all need never present a problem in the Canary Islands. This is self-evident for those travelling to the quiet islands of El Hierro, La Palma, and La Gomera, but even on the major resort islands it is true. The very fact that mega-resorts have been built on the south coasts of Tenerife and Gran Canaria means that tourism is contained within well-defined limits.

Sand, water, and solitude not far from the seashore

Adventure Excursions
Jeep Safaris
If you want to get off the main roads and see the landscape, you might consider joining a jeep safari. The best of these explore tracks which most hired cars fear (or are simply unable) to tread. There are drawbacks, however. The back of a jeep is hard, cramped, and particularly uncomfortable in inclement weather, and also, even in mildly hot weather, you run the risk of returning badly sunburned and very dehydrated. Many people are known to have spent the following days in bed! It's also impossible for a tour leader to give a running commentary. Some jeep safaris let their clients drive. If you want to try your four-wheel drive skills this may be fine, but you may not be so happy being driven at high speeds over rough ground by a novice whom you have never met before! Jeep excursions are available on all the islands (except El Hierro) through a number of operators, and are widely advertised.

Boat Safaris
Boat trips (or 'safaris') are widely available from most of the larger tourist resorts, and can be a good way to see a different aspect of an island. However, you should always find out what you are letting yourself in for in advance. Do you really want 'free' wine and 'pirate games', or would you prefer coastal views and undisturbed relaxation?

A bewildering variety of craft is available – sailing yachts, large motor launches, small motor launches, glass-hulled catamarans, and the antique *Nostramo*, built in 1919.

If you would prefer to skipper your own course, it's easy to charter a boat from pleasure marinas or yacht clubs (*club náuticos*). (*See pp154–7 for the major centres.*)

The most interesting boat safaris depart from southern Tenerife and Gran Canaria in search of dolphins and whales off the southwest coast. Some 200 short-finned pilot whales live and breed just offshore, and these can normally be seen together with bottle-nosed dolphins.

Submarine excursions, which depart from Puerto Mogán, Gran Canaria, and Las Galletas, Tenerife, should be taken for what they are – pure gimmicks. The authentic miniature submarines, do offers a novel experience but, aside from specially placed wrecks and a few fish, there is little to see – and the submarine nights are very expensive.

Horse Riding
This is a near-perfect way to get off the beaten track, with excursions both inland and along deserted beaches. The following establish-ments offer tuition:

LANZAROTE
Lanzarote a Caballo
Near Uga, on the Arrecife–Yaiza road, Lanzarote. Tel: (928) 173512.
Rancho Texas Equestrian Centre *Puerto del Carmen (signs from Playa de los Pocillos beach). Tel: (928) 173512.*

GRAN CANARIA
Rancho Park
Near Palmitos Parque; Bandama Golf Club Riding School, near Las Palmas. Tel: (928) 351290. **Maspalomas Oasis Riding School**
Tel: (928) 772404.

El Salobre Riding School
Off the Palmitos Park road towards Tablero. Tel: (928) 140378; mobile: (669) 795757; email: hipicachs@eresmas.com canyonhorsefarm@tera.es

TENERIFE
El Rodeo de la Paja
El Ortigal, between La Laguna and La Esperanza, instruction only in Spanish. Tel: (922) 257092.

Bottle-nosed dolphins are a common sight in Tenerife waters

Las Cañadas National Park, Tenerife

Beaches

Conventional wisdom suggests that you need a four-wheel drive vehicle to find the away-from-it-all beaches. However, this is not always the case. One of the finest beaches in all the islands, Playa de las Teresitas at Santa Cruz on the main coast road of Tenerife, is quiet for most of the year. Fuerteventura is a beach-bum's paradise, with mile upon mile of golden sands allowing space for everyone. But if you find yourself on a solitary beach, particularly one facing north or west (this applies to all the islands), swim with great caution, if at all. Currents can be treacherous, and a number of holidaymakers seeking solitude on the west coast of Fuerteventura have come to grief.

Nature lovers can take cover among the dunes either at Maspalomas on Gran Canaria, or at Corralejo on Fuerteventura. Some of the Papagayo beaches on Lanzarote are also known for baring it all, although these can get crowded. While on Tenerife, Los Gaviotas, next to Playa de las Teresitas, is also a beach for naturalists.

The beaches on La Graciosa and Los Lobos are also recommended for escaping the crowds.

Islets

Most holiday guides will tell you there are seven Canary Islands – in fact, there are 13. Among the tiny islands are Los Lobos (north of Fuerteventura), Isla Graciosa, Montaña Clara, and Alegranza, all north of Lanzarote; the two rocky islets of Roque del Oeste and Roque del Este are in the province of Las Palmas.

Regular ferries run to and from Los Lobos and Graciosa. You can walk round Los Lobos in just over two hours.

Aside from other curious tourists, you won't see a soul, as no one lives here. The main attraction is the beach and a pretty lagoon. Don't forget your picnic. By comparison, Graciosa (*see p73*) is positively throbbing. There are two tiny settlements here, and you can even stay overnight in a pension. The beach here is superb.

To get to the tiny other island rocks (further north), you will need an accommodating fishing boat. Ask on Graciosa or at Orzola on Lanzarote. Alegranza is approximately half the size of Graciosa, at 10 sq km, and lies 20km off the north coast of Lanzarote. There is a tiny fishing community here but unless you're a birdwatcher you may well wonder why the island was so named (Alegranza means 'joy').

Montaña Clara (just off Graciosa) is the smallest of all at just 1sq km. It's also the most spectacular, with a 256-m high volcano at its heart.

Mountain Bikes

These are available for hire from most major resorts. Only the very fit will attempt the mountainous inland routes, but Lanzarote and Fuerteventura in particular offer a reasonable amount of flat terrain to explore.

On Tenerife, group cycling tours occasionally depart from the Hotel Tigaiga.

Walking

As more and more inquisitive travellers drive hired cars to every corner of each island, it soon becomes apparent that the only way to leave the crowds behind is to walk. At first sight, the Canaries may not seem ideal for the casual walker. The terrain is often daunting, most islands are not waymarked, and there are few walking tour guides to help you. But don't be put off. One of the best-kept secrets on the islands is the free national park walking tour service provided by ICONA, the Spanish nature conservancy organisation. Just telephone ahead to book your place, and you can enjoy an insider's view of some of the finest scenery on Lanzarote (Timanfaya, *pp70–71, pp80–81*), Tenerife (Mount Teide, *pp90–91*), La Gomera (Garajonay, *p111*), and La Palma (Caldera de Taburiente, *pp126–7*).

See under individual entries for telephone numbers and meeting points. The National Park information offices on Tenerife, La Gomera, and La Palma can also supply maps with footpaths for independent exploration.

A quiet beach on Fuerteventura with Los Lobos in the background

Walking Tours

Surprisingly, there are very few commercial walking tour operators on the islands. **Ecological Tours**, on Gran Canaria, lay on a whole day of three easy treks for walkers of all abilities. The programme varies, but usually starts with an introduction to the island's flora via a gentle walk around the Jardín Canario near Las Palmas; then it's a trek down into the Caldera de Bandama (*see pp50–51*), and after lunch a marvellous scenic walk on one of the island's ancient footpaths near Santa Lucía. (*Book through* **Viajes Drago**, *Edificio Excelsior, Playa del Inglés. Tel: (928) 766490.*)

Gomera Safari can be found in the shopping arcade of the Hotel Tecina at Playa Santiago (*tel: (928) 895100*). They usually include the picturesque 3–4 hour walk from the Roque de Agando to Benchijigua in their programme. On Tenerife you can join the German-led tour group, **Wandern mit Gregorio** (Walks with Gregorio), who depart from the Hotel Tigaiga, Puerto de la Cruz, on both walking and cycling tours. (*Call the hotel for details, tel: (922) 383500; fax: (922) 384055.*)

ICONA on Tenerife publishes a series of walking maps, detailing up to nine walks per map with directions in several languages (including English) – available free from tourist offices. These are not very detailed, but the trails are waymarked – look out for the rustic wooden *Sendero Turistico* (Tourist Footpath) signs.

Tenerife leads the way in signposting walks, and a favourite easy signed walk is the **Barranco del Infierno** near Adeje

Island walk near Santa Lucia, Gran Canaria

(*see p100*). There are also plans here and on Gran Canaria to renovate and open up to the public ancient walkways which criss-cross the island. In Gran Canaria, there are now guided walks three times a week with tour guides. (*Departure: 10am Mon, Wed & Fri, return 6pm. Tel: (689) 775034; or phone Cabildo tourist information: Tel: (928) 264623.*)

As a general rule, the best walking is always to be found in the north and centre of the islands; the south is usually too hot and too dry. You'll need stout walking shoes (boots are best) for walks of any length, plus water, sunhat, and warm clothing if you are walking at high altitudes. Never walk alone, and always tell someone when you expect to be back.

Over the dunes of Maspalomas

Shopping

The first lesson to learn when shopping in the Canaries is to take all those 'tax-free' and 'duty-free' signs with a pinch of salt. The islands were declared a duty-free zone in 1852 by the Spanish authorities in order to stimulate trade, and ever since then they have retained certain privileges (they are now in fact a 'trade-free' zone, which means they are free of certain import taxes), but these benefits are not necessarily all passed on to the customer.

Venerable shop front, Santa Cruz de Tenerife

The luxury goods on which favourable tax rates apply are typically electrical items, cameras, calculators, jewellery, perfume, leather goods, and tobacco and spirits. The last two items are certainly bargains, but elsewhere there is often little to choose between Canarian retailers and keen international airport duty-free shop prices.

Island Goods

There is no doubt that the most satisfying purchases are of those traditional wares made on the islands, sometimes right before your eyes: basketry, wood carvings, pottery, rugs, and embroidered tableware. You will find *centros artesanías* (craft workshops) throughout the islands but, despite their often rustic nature, their wares are not always cheap. This is because many hours' labour go into them (unlike the machine-produced Far East imports you will see sold on the streets, and in some shops).

Canarian consumables which make interesting presents or tasty souvenirs include *mojo* sauces (*see p162*) in small gift packs, and wines you can sample in the *bodegas* of Lanzarote or La Palma. Cigars are also a speciality of La Palma, with large Havana-style torpedoes in foil and wooden boxes, making eye-catching and high-quality presents. These compare very favourably with the best Cuban cigars.

A bunch of *strelitzias* (*see pp92–3*) is an exotic way of saying it with flowers. Florists will box these for you so that they may go straight into the aircraft hold (or you can buy them from street sellers, unboxed, at half the price). *Strelitzias* are hardy travellers and will last for a good number of weeks once cut. Dragon tree seeds are available at the shop in Icod de los Vinos next to the tree (*see p92*).

Markets

The most colourful shopping in the Canaries takes place on a Sunday morning. Each of the two provincial capitals of Santa Cruz (Tenerife) and Las Palmas (Gran Canaria) stages a bustling *rastro* (flea-market) with a strong African influence. On Lanzarote, everyone descends on the Sunday market at Teguise. Eclectic is the only way to describe the range of goods on offer at these jamborees. The event, particularly at Teguise which is something of a carnival, is as important as the merchandise.

The best daily markets are also held in the capitals. Nuestra Señora de Africa, at Santa Cruz, is an attraction in its own right, while the sea-front market hall in the Triana area of Las Palmas is the oldest in the Canaries. Gran Canaria also stages notable Sunday markets at San Mateo and Teror.

Other popular markets include the Mercadillo La Havana in La Orotava, Tenerife (on the terrace above the bus station) on Saturdays (9am–3pm), which sells antiques, crafts, and leather goods.

Ask at the tourist office for details of local market days, particularly if you are self-catering.

Shops

Normal shop opening hours are Monday to Saturday 9am or 10am to 1pm or 2 pm, and 4pm or 5pm to 7pm or 8pm. In resorts, some shops and supermarkets may stay open all day. All the shops listed below are open during these times unless otherwise stated.

Where to Buy
GRAN CANARIA

Las Palmas is the 'duty-free' mecca of the Canaries. If you can't find the camera you want at a competitive price in the maze of shops between Santa Catalina Parque and the beach, you probably won't find it anywhere. For a classier range of shops, including branches of two of Spain's best department stores, look on the Avenida de Mesa y López. At the other end of town, more department stores and antique shops can be found on Calle Mayor Triana.

Up-market shopping on the Avenida de Mesa y López, Las Palmas (Gran Canaria)

Fresh fish on sale in the Mercado de Nuestra Señora de Africa, Santa Cruz de Tenerife

alternative feel. For a windy day's play on the dunes, visit the kite shop.

LANZAROTE

Teguise is undoubtedly the island's most interesting shopping experience, on and off market days (*see p142*). Elsewhere, the island lives up to its tasteful arty image with a variety of designer goods, and its famous wines can be sampled and bought from *bodegas* in La Geria.

TENERIFE

Santa Cruz runs Las Palmas close for its 'duty-free' goods, and the shops in the traffic-free central area of Plaza de la Candelaria, Béthencourt Alfonso, and Calle del Castillo are very popular.

Puerto de la Cruz has interesting shops in its centre, and neighbouring La Orotava combines shopping with sightseeing and craft heritage centres. Shopping opportunities in the south of the island are generally poor.

LA GOMERA/LA PALMA/EL HIERRO

There are few shops on these islands. Look for local wines and liqueurs, palm-honey (*see p163*), Guanche-style pottery, and handicrafts.

What to Buy
GRAN CANARIA
Galeria de Arte, Fataga
Unusual local pottery and good paintings.
Calle Rios, village centre.
Tel: (928) 798207.
El Corte Inglés, Las Palmas
The doyen of Spanish department stores; everything from cheap electrical goods to exclusive designer clothes.

The south is well supplied with shops. The resorts have many ugly *centros commerciales* (shopping centres), where some good bargains and tourist memorabilia can be found

FUERTEVENTURA

The best shopping is to be found in the small shops around the square in Corralejo. Some of these have an ethnic-

Avenida Mesa y López.
Tel: (928) 275408.
Open: all day Mon–Sat.
Tienda de Playa del
Inglés, Playa del Inglés
A craft initiative featuring
the work of potters,
woodworkers, and other
artisans.
Avenida de España, tourist
office. Tel: (928) 720532.
Also at Cruz de Tejeda
(no telephone).

LA PALMA
El Molino, Hoya de Mazo
Pottery workshop
producing high-quality
Guanche-inspired wares.
Carretera Hoya de Mazo.
Open: daily 9am–1pm &
4–8pm. Tel: (922) 440213.

LANZAROTE
Fundación César
Manrique, Taro de
Tahíche
Manrique T-shirts, prints,
posters, and sweatshirts.
Taro de Tahíche.
Tel: (928) 843138 &
843463.
Centro Artesanía de
Haría, Haría
Textiles, including
exquisite lace-work,
pottery, and basket
weaving.
Calle Barranco 4.
Open: Tue–Fri 10am–
1pm, Mon & Sat 10am–
1pm & 4–6.30pm.

Centro Natural, Teguise
Antiques, jewellery,
alternative lifestyle and
beauty products in an
historic building.
Plaza 18 de Julio.
Tel: (928) 845502.
Closed: Sat.

TENERIFE
Centro de Artesanía El
Limonero, Garachico
Charming courtyard
where potters, weavers,
instrument-makers, and
others demonstrate
their skills and sell
their goods.
Avenida Marítima
(opposite Castillo de San
Miguel). No telephone.
Salon Canario del Vino,
Icod de los Vinos
Excellent range of

Canarian wines, both
local and from other
islands, plus cheese,
pastries, and liquors.
Free tastings.
Plaza de la Pilar 5.
La Casa de los Balcones,
La Orotava
Spectacular historic
building with large range
of craft and souvenir
items – embroidery a
speciality.
Calle de San Francisco.
Tel: (922) 382855.
Closed: Sat afternoon.
Casa Touristica,
La Orotava
Embroidered tableware
and souvenirs in an
historic setting.
Calle Iriarte.
No telephone.
Open: 9am–6pm.

Checking out a bargain at the Teguise Market, Lanzarote

Entertainment

You're never short on quantity of entertainment in the larger resort areas, but quality and variety is invariably disappointing. It is often a choice between uninspired international cabaret shows, and grotesque home-from-home 'fun pubs'. If you want something more, and you are looking for something that is locally inspired, you will have a long search. Smaller resorts are more conducive to the sorts of bars and restaurants where a Spanish guitarist may strike up, but even these are few and far between.

The resort of Playa de las Américas (Tenerife), one of the main nightlife zones in the islands

The free *Canary Island Gazette* for Tenerife and Lanzarote makes entertainment suggestions, but the tourist office is your only guide on Gran Canaria. If you're staying on the other islands, what limited nightlife there is usually revolves around the larger hotels.

Casinos

Each of the three important tourist islands has at least one casino. The grandest and oldest is the **Casino Taoro**, perched high in its own landscaped grounds above Puerto de la Cruz on Tenerife (*tel: (922) 380550*). It's the sort of place where you might expect to meet James Bond during one of his thrilling escapades.

Other casinos are the **Casino Santa Cruz** in the Hotel Mencey, Santa Cruz (*tel: (922) 276700/290740*), and the **Casino de Juego** in the Gran Tinerfe Hotel, Playa de las Américas (*tel: (922) 793758*).

Gran Canaria also has a casino in an impressive setting: the **Las Palmas**

Casino in the Santa Catalina Hotel in Doramas Parque (*tel: (928) 243040*). The **Casino Gran Canaria** in the Hotel Meliá Tamarindos in San Agustín (*tel: (928) 774090/762724; casinogc@intercom.es*), and the **Oasis Gran Casino** in the Hotel Oasis, Costa Teguise, Lanzarote (*tel: (928) 590410*) both reside in plush, modern hotels. Also in Lanzarote is the **Centro Ocío**, Avenida de las Playas 12 (*tel: (928) 515000*).

French and American roulette, blackjack, and craps are the most common games. The rules are explained in detail every night before each session (from around 8pm–5am), though neither the fear of losing nor the late hours should stop you from playing. Two common-sense rules to cut your losses are to decide on your limit in advance and stick to it rigidly, and leave your credit cards at the hotel.

You will need your passport, and you must be dressed smartly (though not necessarily in jacket and tie) to be allowed admission.

Discotheques

The epicentres of the islands' pulsating 18–30 nightlife are **Playa de las Américas** (Tenerife) and **Playa del Inglés** (Gran Canaria). The Verónicas area of Playa de las Américas is notorious for attracting more than its fair share of trouble.

Elsewhere, Puerto de la Cruz (Tenerife), Puerto Rico (Gran Canaria), and Puerto del Carmen (Lanzarote) provide the best choice of *discotecas*. If there is an admission charge, then it will normally cover the first drink. Most stay open until 3am, but some *discotecas* go on much later.

The establishments listed on the following pages are among the best of the current crop, and have been popular for some time.

Playa de las Américas presents a mesmerising show of nightclub neon

GRAN CANARIA
Dino's, Las Palmas
Los Bardinos Hotel, Calle Eduardo Benot.

LANZAROTE
Joker, Puerto del Carmen
Avenida de las Playas.

TENERIFE
Bugatti's, Playa de las Américas
Opposite Mediterranean Palace Hotel in Tenerife Royal Gardens.
El Coto Up & Down, Puerto de la Cruz
Oro Negro Hotel, Avenida de Colón.
Victoria, Puerto de la Cruz
Avenida de Colón.

Shows
The only common denominator between the following *espectáculos* (show-spectaculars) is a no-frills, robust attitude to tourist family entertainment. Some of the most popular shows are on tour operators' programmes. Prices are the same everywhere.

GRAN CANARIA
Sioux City
A wild west barbecue and saloon show.
Cañón del Aguila, San Agustín, Gran Canaria.

Tel: (928) 762573/762982; fax: (928)767201; alfredo@encomix.es

TENERIFE
Castillo San Miguel
A night of medieval-style jousting is combined (rather incongruously) with the crooning of the famous 1960s pop stars, the Drifters.
San Miguel Aldea Blanca, 15km east of Playa de las Américas.
Tel: (928) 700276.
Fiesta Canaria Carnaval
The next best thing to the real *Carnaval* (*see pp20–21*), plus Canarian folklore.
Calle Las Toscas, Santa Catalina, Tacoronte (no telephone). Refer to travel agents.

Flamenco
Though it has nothing to do with the Canaries, flamenco shows are regularly staged by the top hotels, and a good flamenco troupe is always a treat. Look too for signs in bars and restaurants. The **Montaña Tropical Centre**, Calle Toscon, Puerto del Carmen, Lanzarote (*tel: (928) 510023*) hosts regular flamenco shows – also staged at **Parque Las**

Américas at Playa de las Américas, Tenerife.

Folklore
Canarian folklore shows are gentle but enjoyable family affairs, with large groups of musicians accompanying a dance troupe in traditional costume. The rhythms are generally Spanish, and played on guitars, flutes, and the *timple*, a small ukulele-like instrument.

The best shows are staged in the **Pueblo Canarios** (Canarian Villages) on Gran Canaria (Doramas Parque, Las Palmas, (*Thu 5pm & Sun 11.30am; tel: (928) 245135*), and Tenerife (*Playa de las Américas, Sun morning*). Worth catching is the Sunday 11 o'clock show at the **Hotel Tigaiga**, Puerto de la Cruz, Tenerife (*tel: (922) 383500; fax: (922) 384055*), which includes a demonstration of *lucha canaria* (Canarian wrestling).

The famous Lanzarote attraction, **Jameos del Agua** (*see p73*), hosts a popular folklore evening every Tuesday, Friday, and Saturday night.
Tel: (928) 848020.

Nightclubs

A nightclub has some element of live entertainment, and usually also provides a full meal as compared with a mere discotheque. The following are among the best, and also feature on most tour operator group excursions.

GRAN CANARIA
Son a Mar (formerly Scala), San Agustín
Probably the biggest and best known show on the islands.
Hotel Meliá Tamarindos. Tel: (928) 774090.

TENERIFE
Andrómeda, Puerto de la Cruz
Flamenco dancers remind you that this is Spanish territory.
Lido Martiánez,
Avenida de Colón. Tel: (928) 383852.

La Cueva, Puerto de la Cruz
An African dance troupe performs African and Hawaiian sets in an old Guanche cave.
Los Realejos, 4km west of Puerto de la Cruz. Tel: (928) 340805.

Performing Arts

The islands are not renowned for their highbrow entertainment, and outside the provincial capitals there is very little in the classical sphere.

Opera and classical music, featuring the Orquesta Sinfónica de Tenerife (Tenerife Symphony Orchestra), may be enjoyed at the **Teatro Guimerá**, Plaza Isla de la Madera, in Santa Cruz (*tickets from Cabildo Insular, Santa Cruz, tel: (922) 239801*).

The performing arts are also well represented in La Laguna and La Orotava, but venues here are not advertised to tourists – look in the local papers for details. In Las Palmas, the major classical venue is the **Teatro Pérez Galdós** (*Calle Lentini 1, tel: (928) 361509; www.culturacanaria.com*). The season is from September to May, though special festivals may take place in high summer.

On Gran Canaria classical guitar performances and recitals are given at the **Insular Tourism Centre** (Avenida España, Playa del Inglés, *tel: (928) 771550*). The new **Auditorio Alfredo Kraus** (Carretera El Rincón, Playa de las Canteras s/n, *tel: (928) 247442; festivaldecanarias. com*) provides an impressive setting for concerts and opera.

Jazz festivals are held in **Puerto de Mogán**, Gran Canaria, in March, and in **La Laguna**, Tenerife (*enquire about dates*).

Folk performers in traditional dress play to Spanish rhythms

Children

Any one of the three major islands can provide an ideal family holiday. In terms of children's activities, Tenerife comes top, followed by Gran Canaria, then Lanzarote. The southern resorts are the best choice on Tenerife and Gran Canaria. Fuerteventura is only recommended if you can make the beach last all day, while the other islands are not geared for children.

The Canarians, like the Spanish, love children, and you will rarely have any trouble taking even small children into restaurants or café-bars.

Go-Karting
Children as young as five can enjoy go-karting, while older kids and parents have their own karts and tracks too (*see* Sport *p159*).

Nightlife
On Tenerife, Castillo San Miguel provides medieval jousting, while on Gran Canaria, Sioux City (good for kids by day too) takes you back to the Wild West. There are several casinos and discotheques, and folklore and flamenco shows are usually never too far away (*see* Entertainment *pp146–9*).

Riding a dromedary on Fuerteventura

MORE KIDS' STUFF

Cable-car to the top of Mount Teide (*see pp90–91*).

Go wild during Carnaval (*see pp20–21*).

Tunnel into the magical Cueva (cave) de los Verdes on Lanzarote (*see p72*).

Have fun at the Maspalomas Holiday World fair (*see p38*).

Visit Montaña Tropical Commercial Centre, Puerto del Carmen on Lanzarote. Enjoy tropical birds, remote-controlled boats, children's shows (Sat 11.30am), and flamenco classes (Sat 12.30pm). Catch a free bus from Avenida de las Playas (*tel: (928) 510582 or (928) 510023*).

Ride a horse or a bike (see *p137 & p139*).

Dive (it's expensive!) with the *Yellow Submarine* (*see p46*).

On Tenerife, look out for the excellent *Totally Curious Children's Guide, Tenerife Explored and Explained* in book shops, or the Cabildo Insular office at Plaza de España, Santa Cruz.

'Safaris'

Choose your mount from camel, donkey, or horse. Camel rides are popular: on Lanzarote in the Montañas del Fuego (*see pp70–71*), on Tenerife at El Tanque, and at Guaza-Arona, on Gran Canaria at Fataga and Maspalomas (*see pp38–41*), and on Fuerteventura at Lajita.

Burros (donkeys) will transport you through the picturesque Barranco de Guayadeque on Gran Canaria (*see p30*). Book through a travel agent. Donkey safaris are also available on Tenerife from El Tanque, and from Arafo (*tel: (922) 500411*). (*See p137 for horse-riding.*)

Whale and dolphin 'safaris' on Tenerife (*see pp136–7*) may well appeal to older children.

Waterparks

None of the four Canarian waterparks is in the Florida-style big league, but **Aguapark Octopus** (*Playa de las Américas, Tenerife, tel: (922) 792266*), **Ocean Park** (*just outside Maspalomas, Gran Canaria, tel: (928) 764361*), and **Aqua Sur**, the biggest waterpark in the Canaries, on the road to Palmitos Park (*bus No. 45 from Maspalomas & No. 70 from Puerto Rico; tel: (928) 140525; fax: (928) 140277*), are deservedly popular with families. **Aguapark Lanza** at Costa Teguise (*tel: (928) 592128; open: Easter–Sep*) serves Lanzarote. (*All open daily from around 10am until 5pm or 6pm.*)

Watersports

If your water babies are old enough to windsurf, you may well be able to find tuition and small boards at one of the many schools on the islands (*see* Sport

pp154–5). Otherwise 'water bananas' and 'ringos' (inflatables pulled behind a speedboat) splash along at Puerto Rico (Gran Canaria), and Playa de las Américas (Tenerife). Pedaloes are also available here and at Puerto del Carmen (Lanzarote).

Wildlife

Tenerife has four bird and wildlife parks. By far the biggest and best is the Florida-style **Loro Parque**, at Puerto de la Cruz (*see p97*). Other island options are **Amazonia** and **Tenerife Zoo and Monkey Park** (both in the south, (*see p101*).

Palmitos Parque is an excellent bird (and butterfly) park on Gran Canaria (*see p42*), as is **Reptilandia** (*see p45*). **Guinate Tropical Bird Park** on Lanzarote is also worth a flying visit (*see p73*) for birdwatchers.

Aguapark Octopus, Tenerife

Architecture

merchant's or colonist's home. The Canaries are famous for their balconies, and many modern buildings try to turn the clock back with handcrafted appendages. The wood comes from the heart of the Canarian pine tree and is known as *tea*.

The first Canarians, the Guanches, had little regard for architectural niceties, using the nearest hole in the wall as a home. Caves at least have the benefit of being cool in summer and warm in winter. Not all Guanches lived in caves, however, and it is quite likely that the first Guanche houses were not unlike the small, white, one-storey dwellings found in the Canarian countryside today. These *pueblo*-style houses are built of wood, rough rubblework stone, sand, and mud. Lanzarote provides the finest examples, trimmed and painted green, their chimneys topped with Moorish-style onion domes.

The Spanish brought colonial-style architecture to the islands, and it still survives in many forms in the older towns of the archipelago. Chief among these is La Laguna, on Tenerife, whose old quarter is a showcase of Spanish-Canarian architecture from the 16th and 17th centuries. Sturdy stone mansions with carved coats of arms and beautifully crafted wooden balconies are the exterior hallmarks of a wealthy

Peer inside the entrance of many an old house and you will find a Moorish-style patio, rich with greenery, perhaps even a fountain and, around the interior, more balconies. The epitome of this style is the Casas de los Balcones in La Orotava, on Tenerife. Elsewhere on Tenerife keep

your eyes open in Santa Cruz, Puerto de la Cruz, and Garachico, and do pay a visit to the Casa de la Carta museum, near Valle de Guerre, and the History Museum in La Laguna. The La Vegueta district of Las Palmas and the provincial town of Teror are the pride of Gran Canaria, and Teguise on Lanzarote, and Santa Cruz de la Palma also feature notable vernacular domestic architecture.

Church architecture on the islands reflects the Spanish, also colonial style, with two splendid examples of *mudéjar* (Moorish-influenced) ceilings in the principal churches of Santa Cruz de La Palma and La Laguna.

A variety of building details: Facing page top: Puerto de la Cruz; below: Betancuria (Fuerteventura); this page top: Santa Cruz (Tenerife); above: Fataga (Gran Canaria); left: Taborno (Tenerife)

Sport and Leisure

The clear, warm waters of the islands and the balmy winter
climate ensure that the Canaries are a favourite year-round
venue for amateur and professional sports enthusiasts.

The windy conditions are a plus factor
for experienced boardsailers, and
Fuerteventura and Tenerife are two of
the world's favourite windsurfing
destinations. But there are plenty of
sheltered bays where, with a little
tuition, beginners can stand upright on
a board or on waterskis. The principal
watersports centre is Puerto Rico on
Gran Canaria, but the south of Tenerife,
Fuerteventura, and Lanzarote also have
much to offer. There are few sporting
facilities (on or off the water) on the
smaller islands.

Sporting opportunities on dry land
are generally not so well developed, but
golfers will not be disappointed by the
quality of courses.

WATERSPORTS
Deep Sea Fishing
Shark, barracuda, swordfish, sailfish,
marlin, tuna, and even stingray are all
on the big-game menu for the fishermen
who charter craft from the many
marinas on the islands. The most
productive fishing grounds are off the
south coast of Gran Canaria, where over
30 world records have been claimed for
various types of fish. If you want to
check out the most successful boats, find
out what time they return to the marina
and see the fishermen pose alongside
their catch for the photo-album picture.
The principal charter marinas are: Gran

Canaria – Las Palmas (Santa Catalina
pier), Pasito Blanco, Puerto Rico;
Fuerteventura – Caleta de Fustes/El
Castillo; Lanzarote – Playa Blanca;
Tenerife – Los Cristianos, Puerto Colón
(Playa de la Américas).

Diving
Diving is very popular in the Canary
Islands because of their warm, clear
waters. Marine life, wrecks, and reefs are
not as prolific here as in other more
exotic diving destinations in the world,
but underwater parks have been
designated at Arinaga, off the east coast
of Gran Canaria, and off both the north
and south coasts of Fuerteventura.
All the following clubs give tuition:

FUERTEVENTURA
Corralejo
Miquel Aballa Dive Center
Muelle de Corralejo.
Tel: (928) 866243.
The Trés Islas Hotel
(tel: (928) 535700), and
Oliva Beach Hotel
(*tel: (928) 866100*) both
organise diving in the
marine park between
Corralejo and Isla de los
Lobos.

Jandía
Aldiana Diving Club
Carretera de Jandía.
Tel: (928) 541447.
Felix (Barakuda) Club
Reef dives twice daily
(for experienced divers).
Tel: (928) 541417.
Sotavento Beach Club
*Urbanización Cañada del
Río, Costa Calma.*
Tel: (928) 547041.

Morro del Jable
Los Sargos Diving Club
Campo de Lucha.

GRAN CANARIA
Las Palmas
Club La Tortuga
Tel: (928) 770218.

Maspalomas
Náutico School
Ifa Faro Hotel,
Tel: (928) 142214.

Playa del Inglés
Padi Diving School
*Hotel Folias, San
Agustín.*
Tel: (928) 763923.
Sun Sub School
*Buenaventura Beach
Hotel. Tel: (928) 761650.*

Puerto de Mogán
Top Diving
Tel: (928) 560609.

LANZAROTE
Costa Teguise
Calipso Diving
*Centro Commercial
Nautical, Avenida de las
Islas Canarias.*
Tel: (928) 590879.
Lanzarote Surf Company
Tel: (928) 592212.
Sport Away
Las Olias 18.
Tel: (928) 590731.

Puerto del Carmen
Atlantic Diving Center
*Apartotel Fariones Playa
2, Calle Acatife.*
Tel: (928) 512755.

TENERIFE
Adeje
Club Barracuda
Hotel Paraíso Floral.
Tel: (922) 740750.

Las Galletas
Coralsub–TenBel
TenBel Hotel Complex.
Tel: (922) 785231.

Playa de las Américas
Park Club Europe
Tenerife
Tel: (922) 757060.

**Centro Insular de
Deportes** is the Tenerife
centre for watersports.
*Tel: (922) 239827 or
(922) 239605.*

Sailing
Boats of various sizes
can be hired from
several sports marinas
(*puerto deportivo*)
around the islands.
Below are some of the
principal marinas, local
sailing clubs, and
federations.

FUERTEVENTURA
Jandía
Aldiana Yacht Club
Hobie Cat sailing.
Carretera de Jandía.
Tel: (928) 541147/48.

GRAN CANARIA
Bahía Felíz
Mistral Club
Tarajalillo Beach.

Las Palmas
Federación de Vela
(Sailing Federation).
Tel: (928) 234769.
Puerto Deportivo
(marina office),
Calle Léon y Castillo.
Tel: (928) 234566.

Real Club Náutico de Gran Canaria
Puerto de la Luz.
Tel: *(928) 234566.*
Real Club Victoria
Paseo de Las Canteras 4.
Tel: *(928) 460630.*

Maspalomas
Catamaran Club
Tel: *(928) 642631.*
Maspalomas Yacht Club
(Pasito Blanco).
Tel: *(928) 142194.*
Puerto Deportivo de Mogán Marina office
Tel: *(928) 565480.*

Playa des Inglés
Timanfaya Sailing
Tel: *(928) 762696.*

Puerto Rico
Wolf Sailing
Puerto Escala.
mobile: *(608) 354169.*
Puerto Deportivo de Puerto Rico
Avenida Doreste y Molina
Tel: *(928) 561141.*

LANZAROTE
Puerto Calero
Marina office
Tel: *(928) 814437.*

TENERIFE
Los Cristianos
Puerto Deportivo Los Cristianos Junta del Puerto *(marina office).*
Tel: *(922) 797863.*

Los Gigantes
Puerto Deportivo Los Gigantes
Oficina del Puerto (marina office).
Tel: *(922) 868022.*

Playa de las Américas
Puerto Deportivo Colón
(marina office).
Tel: *(922) 714211.*

Santa Cruz
Real Club Náutico de Tenerife
Avenida de Anaga.
Tel: *(922) 243520.*

Surfing
There is very little organised surfing in the Canaries. It's normally the preserve of the locals who brave dangerous seas and currents. Never surf alone. The best locations include: Gran Canaria – Maspalomas Beach, and Puerto Rico; Fuerteventura – Isla de los Lobos; Lanzarote – Playa Famara and Playa Martiánez (Puerto de la Cruz).

Waterskiing
All the following places offer waterskiing and jet skiing; some also do parascending.

FUERTEVENTURA
Corralejo Beach.

GRAN CANARIA
Puerto Rico Waterski School
Tel: *(928) 735656.*

LANZAROTE
Costa Teguise
Lanzarote Surf Company
Playa Las Cucharas.
Tel: *(928) 346022.*

Playa Blanca
Los Delfines Watersports
Playa Dorada, next to Hotel Playa Dorada.

Puerto del Carmen
Fariones Beach.

TENERIFE
Playa de Las Américas.

Windsurfing
A very popular sport practised off almost any beach. The following are only the main centres, where tuition is available. (*See pp60–61.*)

FUERTEVENTURA
Caleta de Fustes/ El Castillo
Fanatic Surf Center
Tel: *(928) 866486.*

Corralejo
Ventura Surf
Tel: *(928) 866295.*

Fanatic Fun Center
Hotel Trés Islas
Tel: (928) 535700.

Costa Calma
Fanatic Fun Center
Playa de Costa Calma,
Hotel Monica beach.
Tel: (928) 547214.

Jandía
F2 Pro Center
Los Gorriones Hotel, Playa
Barca. Tel: (928) 547202.
Robinson Club
Playa de Matorral.
Tel: (928) 541375.
Bahía Sports
Mancha 20.
Tel: (928) 532226.

Aldiana Yacht Club
(see Sailing*).*

GRAN CANARIA
Las Palmas
Playa de las Canteras.
Tel/fax: (928) 140795.

Maspalomas
Dunkerbeck F2
Windsurfing School
Tel/fax: (928) 762958.
Passat School
Aguila Beach (also at Playa
del Inglés), Maspalomas.

Puerto Rico
Sailing School
Puerto Escala.
Tel: (928) 565292.

LANZAROTE
Costa Teguise
Lanzarote Surf Company
Playa Las Cucharas.
Tel: (928) 591974.
International
Windsurfing Centre
Playa Las Cucharas.

Playa Blanca
Playa Dorada.

Puerto del Carmen
Los Fariones
Playa de los Pocillos and
Matagorda.

TENERIFE
Playa de las Américas.
Opposite Palm Beach Club.

Plenty of surf for the daring

JUMP TO IT!

*P*arapente (para-gliding) is a relatively new Canary Island sport, similar to hang-gliding, but using a parachute-like wing. If you would like to fling yourself off a Tenerife hillside and man your own flight, contact: Club Parapente Guelillas in Santa Cruz, Tenerife. *Tel: (922) 551764.*

LAND SPORTS – PARTICIPATORY

Cycling

Mountain bikes are widely available for hire from major resorts on Gran Canaria, Fuerteventura, Lanzarote, and Tenerife.

Golf

There is still only a handful of clubs on the islands, but quality is good. All the following have a driving range, practice putting green, club and trolley hire, and club house.

FUERTEVENTURA

El Castillo/Antigua

18-hole course, set in a beautiful hotel complex with modern facilites.
El Castillo s/n.
Tel: (928) 174365.

GRAN CANARIA

Campo de Golf Maspalomas

Beautiful location on the edge of the dunes and the oasis. 18 holes, 6,216m.
Avenida TO Neckermann.
Tel: (928) 762581.

Cortijo Club Decampo

This brand new 18-hole course is 6km from Las Palmas, and 10 minutes from the airport.
Autopista GS 1km 6, 4 Telde. Tel: (928) 684890.

Real Club de Golf de Las Palmas (Club Bandama)

This century-old club was the first ever to be formed on Spanish territory, and enjoys a magnificent setting on the edge of the Caldera de Bandama. 18 holes, 5,679m.
Santa Brígida, 14km southwest of Las Palmas.
Tel: (928) 354991.

Salobre Golf

18-hole course nestled in the hills behind Pasito Blanco.
Autopista GC 1km 53.
Tel: (928) 010103.

LANZAROTE

Club de Golf de Costa Teguise

Handicap required: 28 men, 32 women. 18 holes.
Avenida de Golf, Costa Teguise. Tel: (928) 590512.

TENERIFE

Golf Club Amarilla

18 holes.
Amarilla Country Club San Miguel de Abona.
Tel: (922) 730319.

Golf del Sur

Home to the Tenerife Open. Handicap necessary. 27 holes.
San Miguel de Abona,

Autopista del Sur, km 61, 5.
Tel: (922) 738943.
Golf Tenerife El Peñón
18 holes, 5,200m.
Tacoronte.
Tel: (922) 636607/636487.

Go-Karting
Tracks vary in speed, size, and facilities. All have karts that range from child- to adult-sized.

GRAN CANARIA
Gran Karting Club
Claimed to be the largest track in the world at 1,650m; also features mini-motorbikes for children aged over 10.
Carretera General del Sur, km 46, Tarajalillo, Maspalomas.
Tel: (928) 157190.

LANZAROTE
Eurokart
San Bartolomé.
Tel: (928) 590028.

TENERIFE
Karting Canarias
Carretera La Esperanza, km 3.5, Los Baldíos.
Tel: (922) 257038.
Karting Club Las Américas
Carretera General del Sur, Adeje. Tel: (922) 713096.

Tennis
Many larger hotels have tennis courts which are hired out to the public. Tennis centres in Tenerife include: Hotel Las Palmeras, where tuition and floodlit courts are available (*tel: (922) 790991*). The TenBel Hotel complex (*tel: (922) 730060),* and Tenisur, San Eugenio (*tel: (922) 796167*) have similar facilities. In Lanzarote is Club La Santa, near Tinajo (*tel: (928) 840101*). In Gran Canaria the Tennis Centre Maspalomas also has gym facilities (*tel: (928) 767447*).

SPECTATOR SPORTS
Football
CD Tenerife, whose home ground is in Santa Cruz, plays in the Spanish 2nd division and has hosted the likes of Barcelona and Real Madrid. Matches are usually on a Saturday evening or a Sunday. See the local papers for details. On Gran Canaria now, VD Las Palmas is in the 1st division.

Sailing (Vela Lateena)
On Gran Canaria, traditional Canarian sailing *lateens* (small crafts with large triangular sails) race off Las Palmas and Puerto Rico on Saturday afternoons and Sunday mornings between April and September.

Wrestling (Lucha Canaria)
This traditional fighting sport is likely to appeal to fans of Sumo wrestling. The basic objective is to throw your opponent to the ground, but there are other rituals to be observed. The sport is active on all the islands and most villages have a team comprising 12 wrestlers.

Club Bandama – Spain's oldest golf course

Café Life

If you want to see real Canarians at play, just walk into any busy café, buy a coffee or a beer and take a ringside seat. Cafés are usually fairly spartan, noisy, recreational meeting areas, male-oriented (although women do go there, too), and tolerant of children any time of day or night.

Spain is known to be one of the noisiest places in the world, and many Canarian cafés seem to take it upon themselves to uphold this tradition. The television can be on from the day's first children's cartoon, through the dreadful afternoon soap operas, to the evening game shows. Hardly anyone is watching, and most probably cannot hear what is going on anyway, owing to the radio behind the bar, or the fruit machine in the corner, filling the whole café with loud electronic tones. No wonder the locals shout and gesticulate at each

other – it's the only way to be heard!

The only time the TV really draws the audience is when a football match is on. CD Tenerife are the local favourites; otherwise the crowd will cheer for Barcelona, or indeed anyone else who will put Real Madrid's nose out of joint.

Locals may add to the cacophony by striking the metal bar with coins to grab the attention of the barmen. Alcoholic drinks are served at any time, in devil-may-care measures, though most locals start the day with a *café solo* (black coffee). Tourists generally order *café con leche* (coffee with milk), while those who want an alternative between harsh black and sweet or milky white, opt for a *cortado* (small with a little milk). *Donuts* (it's the same word) and *tostada* (toast) are usually available for breakfast. After a quick scan of the papers and a word to their friends,

those who have work to go to, depart. Those who don't, and the older retired men, sit down for a game of dominoes or cards; and around midday the *tapas* (a quarter of a portion of a normal meal) is unveiled and eaten.

At the heart of daily life are the cafés – nearly always well populated by locals, whatever the time of day

Food and Drink

Canarian food is tasty, fresh and filling, though rarely glamorous. Unfortunately, on the larger islands, it's usually easier to find a 'Real British Pub' or a fast-food restaurant than a Canarian *tipico* (typical native restaurant). The latter is distinguished by a relatively short menu of soups, stews, and grilled fish dishes. If you can't find a *tipico*, the best alternative for local food is a place serving *tapas*. This is the Spanish custom of serving small portions of local food in informal restaurant or bar surroundings. *Tapas* bars, however, are also quite thin on the ground in the tourist centres.

Locally produced goats' milk cheese is definitely worth sampling

Canarian Cuisine

Canarian cuisine is essentially peasant and fishermen's food. Meat usually features as part of a stew (normally pork, veal, or rabbit). Steaks, generally imported from Spain or South America, are for tourists only.

Soupy stews are the most typical Canarian meals. *Potaje* has only vegetables; add meat to make *rancho canario,* and add more meat still to make *puchero.* This is, of course, a generalisation; each is flavoured differently, with herbs such as thyme, saffron, marjoram, parsley, and particularly cumin and coriander, but basic ingredients are similar. A Guanche staple, *gofio* (maize meal), once eaten as bread, is still used to thicken stews. Another common stew is *garbanzo compuesto* (chick-pea stew with meat), often available as a *tapas.*

Other typical Canarian casserole dishes are *sancocho,* a stew of salted fish (often seabass), and *conejo con salmorejo* (rabbit in a spicy, tomato-based sauce).

Fresh fish is always on the menu, and seaside restaurants can offer a bewildering and untranslatable fish list (although it's rarely the case that everything listed on the menu is available). The method of cooking is usually plain – either boiled, fried, or grilled (often on a barbecue). As an accompaniment you will be served salad and *papas arrugadas* ('wrinkled potatoes'). The latter are small potatoes, boiled in their jackets in very salty water. On the table there will be two cold olive oil-based sauces; red *mojo picón* (piquant sauce) and *mojo verde* (green sauce). The latter is a cool parsley and coriander sauce, perfect with fish; the former is a spicy chilli and paprika mix, generally poured over potatoes and/or red meat.

The most famous Canarian dessert is *bienmesabe*, a concoction of honey, almonds, and rum. Despite its frequent appearance on menus, it is rarely available, and you may have to make do with the ubiquitous Spanish flan (a cooked milk dessert, like crème caramel).

Do try the local cheese, wherever you are. This is always made from goats' milk, and is invariably good.

Drinks

Lanzarote and La Palma are famous for their Malvasia-style wines, grown on the volcanic soil. These come in dry as well as sweet styles, and are good quality, the best being rich and full-bodied.

Canarian after-dinner drinks include *mistel* (a sweet wine), and *parra* (a firewater-style *aguardiente* brandy), though these are not common. *Ronmiel* (rum-honey) is to be found everywhere. White cane-spirit rum is made on Gran Canaria; the 'honey' is actually sap from the palm tree, gathered in La Gomera. The resultant cocktail is a pleasant, smooth, orange-tasting drink, resembling neither conventional rum nor honey!

Sancocho

This is a popular dish with the Canarians, made up of herbs, salted fish, sweet potatoes, and vegetables, all cooked together.

Papas Arrugadas (wrinkled potatoes). Small potatoes in their skins are boiled with rock salt (a lot) and then served with hot paprika, with chilli sauce poured over them.

The sea's bountiful harvests provide the base for much of the local cuisine

Where to Eat

Eating out is relatively inexpensive. In the resorts, competition tends to keep prices down, and in the villages, eating out is generally priced for the locals. If you don't mind fairly basic amenities and a menu with little choice, and you can manage a little Spanish, the latter is nearly always better value and more enjoyable. Portions are usually large, and a typical Canarian soup-stew starter may well suffice as a main course.

In the listings of recommended restaurants the approximate cost of a three-course meal per person with a half-bottle of wine, or a couple of beers, is indicated by the following symbols:

★	€ 7.5–10.5
★★	€ 10.5–15
★★★	€ 15–21
★★★★	over € 21

EL HIERRO
Mirador de la Peña ★★
Canarian and island specialities are served in tranquil surroundings, with panoramic views.
Guarazoca
Tel: (922) 550300.

FUERTEVENTURA
Antigua
El Molino ★★
Fuerteventuran specialities are served in an atmospheric former granary building.
Carretera del Sur, km 19.
Tel: (928) 878220.

Corralejo
La Marquesina ★★
Locals and tourists mix in this unpretentious harbourside fish restaurant.
Muelle Viejo, old town harbour. Tel: (928) 535435.

GRAN CANARIA
Cruz de Tejeda
Restaurante Asador Grill Yolanda ★★
Excellent and inventive Canarian specialities served in this typical Canarian restaurant.
Tel: (928) 666276.

Las Palmas and Environs
Ca'Cho Damian ★★
Canarian cuisine includes tasty soups. Long bar serving variety of *tapas*.
Centro Comerical La Ballena 26–28.
Tel: (928) 365323/417300.
El Cerdo Que Rie ★★
Convivial basement restaurant, famous for its Spanish food, fondues, and flambés.
Paseo de Las Canteras, 31 (no telephone).
La Parilla ★★★★
Superb international cuisine in this 5-star hotel.
Hotel Reina Isabel, Calle Alfredo L Jones 40.
Tel: (928) 260100.
Playa de Arinaga
La Farola ★★/★★★
Excellent fresh fish.
Tel: (928) 180410/180224.

Tipico in the Edificio Rincon del Puerto, Puerto de la Cruz (Tenerife)

A typical counter display to tempt the tastebuds

Maspalomas
Orangerie ★★★
A creative blend of
Canarian, Spanish, and
international styles.
Palm Beach Hotel,
Avenida del Oasis.
Tel: (928) 140806/721032.

Mogan
Acaymo ★★
Excellent rustic
restaurant serving
Canarian specialities.
Calle San José, Mogán.
Tel: (928) 569263.

Playa del Inglés
La Toja ★★★
Small, pleasant restaurant,
superb Galician dishes.
Edificio Barbados,
Avenida de Tirajana.
Tel: (928) 761196.

Tenderete II ★★
Canarian cuisine with
seafood specials served in
simple, attractive
surroundings.
Avenida de Tirajana
Tel: (928) 761460.
Toro Negro II ★★/★★★
This restaurant
overlooks the beach,
and serves some of the
best Canarian food in
the south.
Centro Comercial
Tropical (near the Hotel
Parque Tropical).
Tel: (928) 766740.

Puerto de las Nieves
Dedo de Dios ★★
Bright, airy fish
restaurant with views of
the impressive Dedo de
Dios rock stack.

The harbour.
Tel: (928) 898000.

LA GOMERA
Las Rosas
Las Rosas ★★
Canarian food, wonderful
views, and a demon-
stration of *el silbo* (*see*
p116); popular with
coach parties. Lunch only.
Carretera General.
Tel: (922) 800916.

Playa de la Santiago
Hotel Jardín
Tecina ★★★★
Request a balcony table
to enjoy excellent
Canarian-international
cuisine, along with a
stupendous view.
Lomada de Tecina.
Tel: (922) 145850.

San Sebastián
Parador Nacional Conde de La Gomera ★★★★
Superb innovative Canarian dishes in a very convincing mock-historic setting.
Balcón de la Ville y Puerto.
Tel: (922) 871100.

LA PALMA
San Nicolás
Bodegón Tamanca ★
Rustic cave bar serving local food in generous helpings.
Las Manchas, 10km south of Los Llanos de Aridane.
Tel: (922) 462155.

Santa Cruz and Environs
Parilla Chipi Chipi ★★
Attractive garden restaurant famous for its barbecued fish and meats.
Los Alamos 42 (Velhoco).
Tel: (922) 417600.

Restaurante Canaria ★
Functional but friendly modern seafront establishment offering good-value Canarian dishes.
Avenida Marítima 28.
Tel: (922) 411000.

LANZAROTE
Costa Teguise
La Chimenea ★★★
Elegant beachside dining from an international

menu. Closed Sunday and July.
Avenida Islas Canarias.
Tel: (928) 590837.

Haria
Mirador de Los Valles ★★
Small, friendly, *mirador* restaurant serving fresh fish and lamb specials. Closed Tuesday.
Los Valles, km 17.8 (south of Haría).
Tel: (928) 528036.

Montañas del Fuego
El Diablo ★★
All cooking is done on the grill above the live volcano. Superb views over the Mountains of Fire.
Islote del Hilario, Parque Nacional de Timanfaya.
Tel: (928) 840057.

Puerto del Carmen
El Sardinero ★★
The town's most famous fish restaurant. Book a first-floor window table to watch the locals playing *boules*.
Plaza El Varadero.
Tel: (928) 511933.

Restaurant las Vegas ★★/★★★
Serves fresh fish and meat in gourmet dishes from the islands.
Avenida Los Palmas.
Tel: (928) 513644.

Teguise
Acatife ★★
Fine Canarian and Spanish specialities are served in a historic setting. Closed Sunday and Monday.
Plaza de la Constitución.
Tel: (928) 845037.

Restaurante Lagomar ★★
This restaurant is situated in an ex-holiday villa of Omar Sharif. It has Canarian dishes very well cooked and served.
Los Loros 6, Nazaret.
Tel: (928) 845665.

Yaiza
La Era ★★
A cute *tipico* known for its Canarian cuisine.
Signposted off Carretera General.
Tel: (928) 830016.

TENERIFE
Cañadas del Teide
Parador de Cañadas del Teide ★★★
The dining room serves superb Canarian dishes.
Parque Nacional del Teide, opposite Los Roques.
Tel: (922) 386415.

Garachico
Isla Baja ★★
A popular fish restaurant, overlooking the front.
Calle Esteban de Ponte 5.
Tel: (922) 830008.

A simply decorated *tipico* in Playa de las Américas (Tenerife)

Los Cristianos
El Bote ★
This tiny boat-shaped bar serves the best *tapas* in Los Cristianos/Playa de las Américas.
Calle El Cabezo (behind the harbour promenade).
No telephone.

El Sol ★★★
Classic French cuisine is prepared by the owner-chef at this popular restaurant.
The port.
Tel: (922) 790569.

Playa de las Américas
El Dornajo ★
A *tipico* where good quality and quantity is supervised by the owner-chef.
Avenida Litoral.
Tel: (922) 791425.

Puerto de la Cruz and Environs
Casa de Miranda ★★★★
Elegant first-floor restaurant in historic 18th-century house. Lighter dishes and *tapas* served in the ground-floor *bodega*.
Calle Santo Domingo 13, Plaza de Europa.
Tel: (922) 373871.

Mario ★★/★★★
Small fish restaurant in the pretty Rincón del Puerto courtyard complex. It is closed on Mondays.
Edificio Rincón del Puerto, Plaza El Charco.
Tel: (922) 385535.

Meson Los Gemelos ★★★
Rustic, cosy interior; specialising in *tapas*, fresh fish, shellfish, and charcoal-grilled meat.
Calle el Peñon 4.
Tel: (922) 370133.

Mi Vaca y Yo ★★★
Charming, typical Canarian rustic setting for excellent local and international cuisine, particularly seafood. Dinner only.
Calle Cruz Verde 3.
Tel: (922) 385247.

Hotels and Accommodation

The vast majority of tourist accommodation in the Canary Islands has been built over the last 20 years to cater for package holidaymakers. This has been mostly concentrated in the large resorts of southern Tenerife and southern Gran Canaria, but the south of Fuerteventura, Costa Teguise, and Puerto del Carmen on Lanzarote have also been built up. The small islands, however, have hardly been touched, so if you want to visit them, book ahead.

The *parador* in the Teide National Park is a comfortable mountain lodge

Unfortunately for independent travellers, there is no tradition of private accommodation (as, for example, in the Greek Islands), nor the small type of family-run hotels that are found in mainland Spain. Only in the older resorts, the two major island capitals, and the odd village here and there, is it possible to find 'unpackaged' accommodation.

Hostales

Hostales, designated by the sign Hs, are of a lower standard than hotels, and are graded from 1 to 3 stars. Facilities in a 3-star *hostal* should be the equivalent of a reasonable 2-star hotel, but don't expect much in 1- or 2-star places. There are very few of these establishments (look in Santa Cruz de Tenerife, El Hierro, and Arrecife, Lanzarote).

Hotels

Pick up any holiday brochure and you will find page upon page of characterless Canarian hotels, all built to a similar 3- or 4-star standard. These provide comfortable, well-equipped rooms, a swimming pool, bars, possibly a discotheque, live nightly entertainments, sports facilities, boutiques, and so on. Many of these are large (around 300 rooms), and high-rise, and a good number are still raw around the edges.

Cheap hotels (below a 3-star grading) are thin on the ground. Try Las Palmas, Santa Cruz de Tenerife, Puerto de la Cruz, and Fuerteventura.

Travellers putting together their own package in 3- or 4-star hotels (or apartments) are advised to book well ahead and shop around for prices.

The hotels' stated nightly rates often bear little resemblance to what may be negotiated. In general, however, it would be difficult to beat the price of a late availability package.

Hotelapartamentos

Hotelapartamentos or aparthotels feature rooms with their own kitchen facilities, yet retain most of the other trappings of an ordinary hotel. These are popular in most large resorts, and a good bet for families with children.

Paradores

Paradores are state-run hotels, renowned for providing the best accommodation available in any particular region of Spain. All the Canary Islands once had *paradores*, but the one on Lanzarote (at Arrecife) closed, and Gran Canaria's *parador* is now just a restaurant. The other five survivors all succeed in their stated aim of reflecting local style and decor, and providing the very best in local and regional cooking.

The days when *paradores* were a cheap way of seeing Spain have long gone. They are now classified like other hotels, from 1 to 5 stars, and they all charge commercial rates.

The best (and most expensive) establishment is the mock-colonial Conde de la Gomera, an attraction in its own right, and recognised as one of the finest small *paradores* in all Spain (*see p112*). The other *paradores* are no less individual. Fuerteventura's modern *parador* at Puerto del Rosario resembles (surely unintentionally) the town's foreign legion barracks, but is really quite comfortable inside; Tenerife's Cañadas del Teide *parador* resembles a mountain chalet, cosy and popular with walkers; Santa Cruz de la Palma's *parador* merges seamlessly with the traditional seafront houses. If you really want to get away from the crowds, El Hierro's modern-traditional *parador*, set at the end of a road going nowhere on the loneliest island of them all, is the last word in solitude. All, apart from Santa Cruz, have their own swimming pools.

For central bookings contact Paradores de Turismo de España, Requena 3, 28013 Madrid (*tel: (91) 515 6666; fax (91) 516 6657*). In the UK contact Keytel International, 402 Edgware Road, London W2 1ED (*tel: (020) 7402 8182*). Enquire at the Spanish National Tourist Office in other countries.

Apartamentos Lanzamar – typical low-rise tourist accommodation on Lanzarote

Pensiones

A *pensión* (guest house) is a relatively rare sight in the islands. The best place to look is in Puerto de la Cruz, Tenerife, where there is a choice of nine. However, by nature, these are very small and, given Puerto's popularity, the best are likely to be booked in advance. Write to the Puerto tourist office (*see p96*) or your own Spanish National Tourist Office for a list of these.

Elsewhere on Tenerife there is a handful of *pensiónes* in Santa Cruz and the smaller towns on the island. There is a choice of six on La Palma. The Pension Cubana in Santa Cruz de La Palma is particularly notable for its excellent state of preservation, its antique furnishings, and its ideal location.

Las Palmas, Gran Canaria, has several *pensiónes,* but only hardy travellers should consider staying in the back streets where some of these are located.

Self-Catering

Self-catering bungalows and apartments are a popular holiday choice in the Canary Islands, and are usually grouped together in developments known as *urbanizaciónes.* These also often include time-share apartments.

If you would like an apartment away from the tourist ghettos, ask the local tourist office for details (many of these are only for rent for a minimum period of a month), or, before you go, consult one of the smaller specialist island operators.

Camping

Given the ideal climate for camping, sites are surprisingly few and far between. There are only three official sites on the islands, but *camping sauvage* (wild camping – off-site) is tolerated in many places. Enquire at the local tourist office to reduce the chance of being moved on by jealous farmers or possessive landowners.

Tenerife has just one official site: the well-equipped Nauta Camping/ Caravanning at Las Galletas, Arona, on the south coast (*tel: (922) 785118*). If you do see backpackers on southern Tenerife it is likely they are off to La Gomera – probably to the Valle Gran Rey, popular with campers and those in search of an alternative lifestyle.

There is one designated site on La Gomera, at Caserio de Cedro on the edge of the Garajonay National Park. This is administered by the island government office, and if you wish to camp here you should contact the office in San Sebastián de La Gomera, Carretera General del Sur 20 (*tel: (922) 870105*).

Camping within the National Park is strictly forbidden on La Gomera, as it is on Tenerife and Lanzarote. Climbers and keen walkers in the Teide National Park, however, may apply to use the spartan mountain refuge at Altavista (contact ICONA, at Calle del Pilar 1, Santa Cruz, Tenerife, *tel: (922) 290129*).

La Palma permits camping in the National Park (maximum stay two nights) as long as permission is sought in advance. The site is below Roque Salvaje (1½–2 hours' walk from Los Brecitos). Apply to Parque Nacional de la Caldera de Taburiente, Calle O'Daly 35, Santa Cruz de la Palma (*tel: (922) 413141*). In the Caldera zone apply at the

Centro de Visitantes in El Paso (*tel: (922) 497277*). For La Laguna de Barlovento and La Fajara, phone the *ayuntamiento* in Barlovento (*tel: (922) 186002*). For the La Rosa area, *tel: (922) 493306*, and for other areas, *tel: (922) 411593*.

Gran Canaria has five sites. The two official ones are Camping Guantánamo at La Playa de Tauro near Puerto Rico (*tel: (928) 560207 or 241701*), and a site at Playa Tauro (*tel: (928) 562075*); another site is at Temisas, Lomo de la Cruz, on the road from Agüimes to San Bartolomé de Tirajana (*tel: (928) 798149*).

All three are well-equipped, but Temisas can only accommodate 50 people. Two unofficial sites are at Pasito Blanco and Fataga (*enquire at the Maspalomas tourist office for details*).

There are no official sites on Fuerteventura, Lanzarote, or El Hierro.

Time Share
Time share is a much maligned accommodation option, largely on account of the unsavoury get-rich-quick characters it seems to attract. Most time-share organisations offer exchange facilities, should you tire of your original choice, or need to change.

There are no specific rules that apply to buying time-share packages in the Canaries that don't apply generally anywhere else. The two golden rules to apply are: never sign anything while on holiday (get home and 'cool off' first), or without sound legal advice. It would also seem common sense to avoid the overtures of the often loutish street-corner touts.

Youth Hostels
There are no youth hostels or similar associations on the islands.

The charming, atmospheric Parador Conde de La Gomera

Tourism

The adverse effects of tourism on the southern coastlines of Gran Canaria and Tenerife are well documented and well discussed. But this does not necessarily mean that lessons have been learned. In fact, the large-scale developments of Jandía on Fuerteventura, and the ridiculously overcrowded bay of Puerto Rico on Gran Canaria argue the reverse. Only Lanzarote and La Palma enforce meaningful controls on tourism development (no advertising hoardings, no high-rise hotels, and so on).

There are, of course, many benefits to the islands and their visitors from the careful development of tourism. The debate goes something like this:

For large-scale development: new roads, hotels, and apartments bring more jobs for the locals (Canarian unemployment was very high); new roads attract visitors to villages, so craft, souvenir, and restaurant premises can thrive; work in tourism is all year round and not subject to the hardship or vicissitudes of farming.

Against large-scale development: hoteliers and time-share operators bring in their own staff and exclude the locals; as young people leave their villages for tourism work, so these settlements are depopulated and die (this in itself is arguably a bad thing, but commercially it is also folly as villages also attract tourists); tourists swamp villages and irrevocably change their character; development brings pollution and destruction of flora and fauna.

A related issue is the direction which tourism should take in the Canaries. Do visitors really want to suffer constant haranguing from time-share touts? The obvious answer is no, and strict regulations have now been passed so that only 'legal time-share representatives' can roam the streets. The 'pile it high and sell it cheap' policy may mean more people in the short term, but the long-term risks are great. The image of the islands has already been badly damaged. While similar islands which cultivate an up-market image (such as Madeira) may perhaps have less to offer than the Canaries, they consistently attract higher-spending tourists who, in the long run, after all, are more profitable.

Profitable operations need not resort to bland international mediocrity, as much of Lanzarote, the island *paradores,* and such establishments as the Hotel Tecina on La Gomera prove. However, with the new building regulations for resort areas coming into force, only 4- and 5-star hotels will now be built, thus improving the overall image, and avoiding a bad reputation.

A burgeoning of tourist accommodation and time-share opportunities has had a dramatic effect on the life of the Canary Islands

On Business

The Canary Islands are no longer the trade hub that their geographical position, halfway between Europe, Africa, and the Americas, once made them. Trade routes have changed, and ships which once stopped here for refuelling and 'rest and recreation' can now sail by, or they have been replaced with air travel, and more fashionable destinations.

Impromptu street business

The island's only business cities are the provincial capitals of Las Palmas and Santa Cruz de Tenerife. Both rely heavily on oil-refining. Santa Cruz is one of the largest refiners in all Spain, processing Venezuelan crude for domestic use. In terms of international trade and commerce, Las Palmas is much more important than Santa Cruz, attracting around 8,000 ships a year. Around five million tons of freight (mostly oil and petroleum) flow in, and one million tons of foodstuffs are exported, mostly to the Spanish mainland.

As part of Spain and therefore a member of the European Union, the islands enforce EU trading conditions. If you require information on any aspect of trading in the Canaries before you depart, write with full details (no telephone requests are dealt with) to: The Spanish Commercial Office, 66 Chiltern Street, London W1M 1PR.

Business Etiquette

Canarians are generally friendly, easy-going people who will often suggest talking business over a slap-up lunch. Don't think this is wasted time or effort. Life is slower here in most aspects than on mainland Europe (although Las Palmas on Gran Canaria is an exception), but don't take this as a sign of provincial naïvety. Many successful businessmen have moved from mainland Spain to the Canaries to facilitate or oversee their import-export trades, and have a keen eye for the next business opportunity.

Business Services

Tenerife, Gran Canaria, and Lanzarote have sizeable expatriate communities (mostly English, but also German and Scandinavian), who supply and use business services. Pick up any of the English-language publications (*see* Media, *p184*) and you will find advertisements for office equipment, secretarial, translation and inter-pretation services, removals and freight, messengers, and all manner of insurance, and financial brokers.

If you are planning to set up your own business on the islands, or to take any legal or financial advice, be very careful. As one of the advertisements frankly admits, 'it's a minefield!'.

One useful publication might be *You and the Law in Spain*, available from Lookout Publications SA, Puebla Lucia, 29460 Fuengirola, Málaga, Spain.

Conferences

For 'olde-worlde' style, the *parador* on La Gomera is a perfect venue, with little to distract delegates from serious business. Another choice on the island is the excellent Hotel Jardín Tecina. A young sales team might appreciate the amusements of Playa de las Américas on Tenerife. There are several hotels with convention halls in the resort. Chief among these is the luxurious Grand Hotel Mediterranean Palace, one of the very few hotels on the islands that actively promote themselves as convention hotels – it is a member of Expo Grupo. Puerto de la Cruz, in the north of the island, is a good halfway house, with traditional class, but plenty of modern amenities too. In Santa Cruz, the only hotel with more than a 3-star rating is the beautiful but expensive 5-star Mencey.

On Gran Canaria there are several large, impressive 4- and 5-star hotels in Las Palmas with conference facilities. The other good place for a serious conference is Maspalomas, with its smart hotels by the oasis, and a new conference centre.

On Lanzarote, Puerto del Carmen and Playa Blanca are possibilities, but the quieter, more up-market Costa Teguise is probably the best bet, particularly if your budget stretches to the Meliá Salinas hotel.

One of the two large hotels on Corralejo beach is the natural choice on Fuerteventura.

The only hotel that a business conference organiser would consider on La Palma is the Sol La Palma at Puerto Naos. If the theme of the conference is getting away from it all, the *parador* on El Hierro is the perfect choice. All of the venues mentioned above are 4-star standard or above, and have a conference hall, but many of them will not be as well equipped with the sound and light facilities that are standard in major world business centres.

Most of the hotels capable of staging conferences belong to groups. Contact them on the following central reservations or head office numbers:
Expo Grupo (Barcelona). *Tel: (933) 259499; fax: (933) 251144.*
Hesperia (Barcelona). *Tel: (932) 650202.*
Iberotel (Majorca). *Tel: (971) 200011.*
Ifa (Gran Canaria). *Tel: (928) 772800.*
NH Hoteles (Barcelona).
Tel: (933) 010000.
Paradores (Madrid). *Tel: (516) 666666 (UK – Keytel International: Tel: (020) 7402 8182).*
Sol/Meliá Hoteles (Majorca).
Tel: (971) 224464.
Tryp Hoteles (Madrid).
Tel: (91) 3153246.

Las Palmas is a bustling commercial city

Practical Guide

Arriving
Visitors from EU countries, the USA, and Canada, need only a passport to enter the Canary Islands. A residence permit or special visa is necessary for stays longer than 90 days.

By Air
There are international airports on Gran Canaria (*tel: (928) 579000*), Fuerteventura (*tel: (928) 860500*), Lanzarote (*tel: (928) 846000*), and Tenerife. Tenerife has two: Tenerife North/Los Rodeos (*tel: (922) 635800/635998*) and Tenerife South/Reina Sofía (*tel: (922) 759200/759000*), which is the main one. Other island airports are: La Gomera (*tel: (922) 873000*), La Palma (*tel: (922) 426100*), and El Hierro (*tel: (922) 553700*).

Regular airport buses go from: Gran Canaria airport to Las Palmas and Maspalomas; from Tenerife South to Los Cristianos/Playa de las Américas/Santa Cruz, and from Tenerife North to Puerto de la Cruz and Santa Cruz. There are also express buses which link Tenerife's two airports. Regular local bus services also run from other island airports. All airports have taxis to meet inter-island flights.

By Boat
There are no regular cruise liner services to the Canaries, although cruise ships do sometimes call at Las Palmas and La Gomera. From mainland Spain, ships sail from Cádiz to Santa Cruz de Tenerife, Las Palmas on Gran Canaria, and to Arrecife on Lanzarote.

Trasmediterránea operates between Cádiz, Tenerife, and Gran Canaria (*see Ferries, p186*).

Camping
Given the scarcity of good, cheap accommodation on the islands, this is one of the few budget options. However, there are few official campsites, but most have good facilities (*see pp170–71*).

Children
The more popular Canary Islands are completely geared for family holidays, and within the major resorts you will find all you need in the way of babycare products. Babysitters can be found for older children, and many hotels have specific children's activities and 'clubs'.

Climate
For all-year-round sunshine you'll have to go to the south of Gran Canaria or the south of Tenerife. The small westerly islands can be quite cool, though for most of the winter they are pleasantly spring-like to North Europeans.

If you're visiting the north of the larger islands, be prepared for some rain and cooler temperatures in the winter. Winds can also be strong. Summer sunshine is virtually guaranteed everywhere.

Conversion Charts
See tables opposite.

Crime
Theft from cars is the most common form of crime against tourists on the islands, with handbag snatching a close

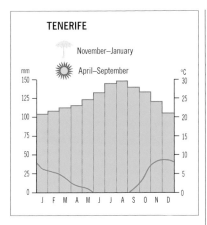

TENERIFE

November–January

April–September

Weather Conversion Chart
25.4mm = 1 inch
°F = 1.8 x °C + 32

Conversion Table		
FROM	TO	MULTIPLY BY
Inches	Centimetres	2.54
Feet	Metres	0.3048
Yards	Metres	0.9144
Miles	Kilometres	1.6090
Acres	Hectares	0.4047
Gallons	Litres	4.5460
Ounces	Grams	28.35
Pounds	Grams	453.6
Pounds	Kilograms	0.4536
Tons	Tonnes	1.0160

To convert back, for example from centimetres to inches, divide by the number in the third column.

second. Never leave anything of value in your car, and make sure it is locked at all times. In contrast to Las Palmas, other Canarian towns and villages are quite safe. However, in tourist areas, keep bags on the side away from the road, and be vigilant.

Hotels usually have safes for hire, although staff are honest and break-ins at good hotels are rare. Apartments are less easy to police.

Violence against tourists is unusual, but don't tempt fate by treading the seamier streets of Las Palmas after dark.

If you are a victim of robbery report the incident to the local police who will give you a copy of your statement for insurance purpose.

Customs Regulations

For customs purposes the Canary Islands are not members of the EU. The duty-free allowance for goods taken in

Men's Suits

UK		36	38	40	42	44	46	48
Rest of Europe	46	48	50	52	54	56	58
US		36	38	40	42	44	46	48

Dress Sizes

UK		8	10	12	14	16	18
France		36	38	40	42	44	46
Italy		38	40	42	44	46	48
Rest of Europe		34	36	38	40	42	44
US		6	8	10	12	14	16

Men's Shirts

UK	14	14.5	15	15.5	16	16.5	17
Rest of Europe	36	37	38	39/40	41	42	43
US	14	14.5	15	15.5	16	16.5	17

Men's Shoes

UK		7	7.5	8.5		9.5	10.5	11
Rest of Europe	41	42	43		44	45	46
US		8	8.5	9.5	10.5	11.5	12

Women's Shoes

UK		4.5	5	5.5	6	6.5	7
Rest of Europe	38	38	39	39	40	41
US		6	6.5	7	7.5	8	8.5

The Tenerife–La Gomera ferry

or out (applicable to persons 17 and over) include: 2 litres of wine; 1 litre of spirits; 200 cigarettes (or 100 cigarillos or 50 cigars or 250g tobacco); 60cc perfume or 250cc toilet water; € 553 worth of gifts per person.

Driving
Car Hire
It is possible to take your own car to the islands via mainland Spain, but as the Canary Islands provide very reasonable car hire rates, it hardly seems worth the effort or expense.

Reliable and competitively priced local firms include **Top-Car Reisen**, with airport offices on Gran Canaria (*tel: (928) 579159; fax: (928) 574746*); in Tenerife North/Los Rodeos (*tel: (922) 262202*); in Tenerife South/Reine Sofia (*tel: (922) 759364*); in Fuerteventura (*tel: (928) 860760; fax: (928) 860762*); and in Lanzarote (*tel: (928) 802753*).

Ciqar Car Hire is also a very good company with the advantage of an office on every island: Lanzarote (*tel: (928) 846266*); La Palma (*tel: (922) 428048*); Fuerteventura (*tel: (928) 846266*); El Hierro (*tel: (922) 551539*); Gran Canaria (*tel: (928) 574424*); La Gomera (*tel: (922) 873031*); Tenerife (South) (*tel: (922) 759329*); and Tenerife (North) (*tel: (922) 632642*).

Should you prefer to book from the UK, try **Hire for Lower**, 25 Savile Row, London W1X 1AA (*tel: (020) 7491 1111*).

Documentation
All British, European, American, and Australian driving licences are valid, although it may be advisable to take a Spanish translation with you (contact a motoring organisation in your own country before travelling). An International Driving Permit is not necessary.

Petrol
Take cash as most petrol stations do not accept credit cards. These are relatively numerous along the main roads, with 24-hour opening in the larger resorts and towns. Don't drive into the mountains on an empty tank, as there are few, if any, filling stations here.

Rules of the Road
Driving is on the right. Seat belts are compulsory in the front and the back. Children under 12 must travel in the back of the car. In towns cars must be parked facing the direction of the movement of traffic. The standard of roads is surprisingly high, with many newly built and very smoothly surfaced.

Motorways (*autopistas*) run along the north and east coast of Tenerife and the east coast of Gran Canaria, connecting airports with major resorts in 30 minutes or less.

The standard of driving is quite reasonable, though do beware of oncoming traffic and impatient drivers on hairpin bends in mountainous areas. Beware of traffic jams in Las Palmas, (Gran Canaria),Puerto de la Cruz and Santa Cruz (Tenerife). Parking is also very difficult in these towns. Las Palmas is particularly bad, though it is sometimes possible to park on the front at Santa Cruz. Beware the fiendish one-way systems in Las Palmas, Puerto de la Cruz, and Arrecife on Lanzarote.

Electricity

The current throughout the islands is 220 volts AC, and sockets take the circular two-pin continental-style plug. If you are out in the wilds, you may rarely find 110 volts supply. Power cuts are infrequent.

Embassies and Consulates

The following addresses are all consulates. Embassies are located in Madrid.

Ireland La Marina 7, Ed Hamilton 6, Santa Cruz, Tenerife. *Tel: (922) 245671.*

UK Plaza de Weyler 8, Santa Cruz, Tenerife. *Tel: (922) 286863*; Edificio Cataluña, Calle de Luis Morote 6, 35007, Las Palmas, Gran Canaria. *Tel: (928) 262508/262658.*

USA Calle Martinez de Escobar, 3 Las Palmas, Gran Canaria. *Tel: (928) 222552.*

Emergency Telephone Numbers

General *061 or 112*

Police (all islands) *091*

Beware of animals crossing your path on Fuerteventura!

Gran Canaria's road signs are works of art

Province of Tenerife
Ambulance (Red Cross):
Tenerife – Santa Cruz: *(922) 281800*;
Puerto de la Cruz: *(922) 383812*;
Los Cristianos: *(922) 753939*;
Las Américas: *(922) 780759.*
Fire Brigade
Tenerife – Santa Cruz: *(922) 606080*;
North: *(922) 328055*;
South: *(922) 735050.*
La Gomera: *(922) 141572.*
La Palma: *(922) 429344.*
El Hierro: *(922) 558176.*

Province of Gran Canaria
Ambulance (Red Cross)
Gran Canaria – Las Palmas: *(928) 222222.* Lanzarote: *(928) 812222.*
Fuerteventura: *(928) 852222.*
Fire Brigade Las Palmas: *080*;
Lanzarote: *(928) 814858*; Playa del
Inglés: *(928) 762671*; Fuerteventura:
(928) 530744.

Loss or Theft of Thomas Cook Traveller's Cheques
Report (within 24 hours) the loss or theft of Thomas Cook Traveller's Cheques, using their 24-hour reverse charges telephone number: *00 44 1733 318950.*

Health
No vaccinations are necessary for a visit to the Canary Islands.

EU citizens can obtain a refund of most medical costs by using form E111 (available from post offices and Health and/or Social Security offices in your own country). If you don't take it, you can still claim back later (remember to keep all receipts). Medical insurance is still strongly advisable.

The most common complaints are stomach upsets caused by a sudden change of diet and too much sun. Break yourself in gradually to sunbathing and always use suntan lotions and blocks. Remember that children are particularly vulnerable.

There are many English-speaking dentists and doctors. Ask your hotel or tourist information office for the nearest one.

Minor ailments can usually be treated at the chemist (*farmacia*). At least one chemist per town or area stays open after hours. Its location is posted in the window of all the other chemists (also available from the tourist office and local newspaper).

Hitch-hiking
This is legal, though not totally safe if you are alone, and with the large number of North European holiday drivers on the roads, not likely to be a quick way of getting around. An official hitch-hiker's card (obtainable

from Youth Hostel Associations) may help.

Lost Property
Lost property offices are few and far between. Ask the tourist office where to go locally. Report lost valuables to the Municipal Police or Guardia Civil and obtain a form for your own holiday insurance purposes.

Maps
As new roads are built so maps go out of date quite rapidly. The AA Macmillan Canary Islands map is recommended. Town plans and basic local maps are usually available from tourist offices.

Media
There are several newspapers and magazines written for the English-speaking visitor to the Canary Islands. Gran Canaria has surprisingly little. In Tenerife look out for the free monthly magazine *Canarian Gazette* and *Tourist Guide Tenerife* and the twice-monthly *Tenerife News.* For Spanish speakers, *La Gaceta de Canarias* and *Diario de Avisos* include useful local listings, in addition to the monthly booklet *LA GUIA – Oció y Cultura* (separate ones for Tenerife and Gran Canaria). Lanzarote offers the *Canary Island Gazette & Tourist Guide.* La Palma has an annual magazine guide, *Guía Practica.* Free magazines are generally available from tourist offices, travel agents, hotels, and popular bars.

All the major international papers are available in the large towns and popular resorts usually the day after publication.

Radio Canarias-Sol provides news and tourist information in English (Mon–Fri 8–8.30am, 3–3.30pm, and 4.30–5pm), and in German at most other times on

The cool, green foliage of a city park provides respite from the hustle and bustle of the streets

LANGUAGE

Canary Islanders speak Spanish, or to be more accurate Castilian (the language of most of mainland Spain). The only real difference that the non-language student will notice is that the letter **c** and **z** are pronounced (softly), instead of lisped with a 'th' sound.

There are a few indigenous words still in use, the most notable being **papa(s)** for potato(es) and **guagua** (pronounced wah-wah) for bus.

It's quite possible in some major resorts to get through two weeks on the islands speaking, and even hearing, nothing other than English. However, off the beaten track, and particularly on the smaller islands, a smattering of Spanish will be helpful if not essential. But wherever you are, your attempts to master a few phrases and, at the very least, daily greetings will always be appreciated.

PRONUNCIATION

Try to remember the following basic rules:

Consonants

c is soft before e and i (eg, Barcelona), but hard at any other time – **como**? (pardon?) pronounced 'ko-mo'.

g at the start of a word is a hard sound (as in get). In the middle of a word it is like the throaty 'ch' as in the Scottish 'loch' – **urgencia** (emergency) is pronounced 'ooer-chensee-ah' In **agua** (water) it is hardly pronounced at all ('ah-kwa').

h is always silent – **hospital** is pronounced 'ospitahl'.

j is also pronounced like the ch in 'loch' – **jamón** (ham) is pronounced 'ch-amon'.

ll is always like 'll' in million – **lleno** (full) is pronounced 'lyay-no'.

ñ is like 'ni' in onion – **España** (Spain) is pronounced 'ay-spanya'.

qu is like k in key – **quánto**? (how much?) is pronounced 'kwan-toe'.

r is rolled: **rr** is rolled even harder.

v is like b in bottle – **vino** (wine) is pronounced 'bee-no'.

x is like s – **excelente** (excellent) is pronounced 'ess-say-len-tay'.

Vowels

a is a short 'ah' sound – **gracias** (thank you). It is never long as in the English 'gracious'. All the other vowels are long sounds. The letter **e** is a cross between the short English e (as in get) and the long English **a** (as in grace) – **de** (of/from) is pronounced 'day' but in a clipped way. The letter **i** is a long 'ee' sound as in sí (yes), pronounced 'see', and **u** is like 'oo' in boot – **una** (one).

DAYS OF THE WEEK	
Sunday	domingo
Monday	lunes
Tuesday	martes
Wednesday	miércoles
Thursday	jueves
Friday	viernes
Saturday	sábado

USEFUL WORDS AND PHRASES

yes/no	sí/no
hello	hola
good morning	buenos días
good afternoon	buenas tardes
goodnight	buenas noches
goodbye	adiós
please	por favor
thank you	gracias
you're welcome	de nada
today	hoy
tomorrow	mañana
yesterday	ayer
I am English	Soy inglés
do you speak English?	¿habla inglés? (informal) ¿habla usted inglés? (formal)
very well/good	muy bien/vale
where is . . ?	¿dónde está . . ?
what/when	qué/cuándo
why/how	por qué/cómo
how much is . . ?	¿cuánto vale/cuesta . . ?
here/there	aquí/ahí
open/closed	abierto/cerrado
right, left	derecho/a, izquierdo/a
sorry!	¡lo siento!
excuse me (can I get past?)	perdóneme
(can you help?)	por favor –
sir, madam, miss	señor, señora, señorita
I don't understand	no comprendo
I would like . . .	quiero/quisiera . . .
large/small	grande/pequeño
do you have . . ?	¿tiene . . ?
please write it down	por favor, escríbalo

NUMBERS

0	cero
1	uno/a
2	dos
3	tres
4	cuatro
5	cinco
6	seis
7	siete
8	ocho
9	nueve
10	diez
11	once
12	doce
13	trece
14	catorce
15	quince
16	dieciséis
17	diecisiete
18	dieciocho
19	diecinueve
20	veinte
21	veintiuno
30	treinta
40	cuarenta
50	cincuenta
60	sesenta
70	setenta
80	ochenta
90	noventa
100	cien/ciento/a
101	ciento uno/a
200	doscientos/as
500	quinientos/as
1000	mil
2000	dos mil
1,000,000	un millón

99.6 FM. Radio Maspalomas has a German programme from 8–9am daily, and an English programme from 9am–10pm daily. It also provides a German language magazine programme from Sunday to Friday 6–8pm on 95.3 FM.

On Tenerife, Canary Island Tourist Radio broadcasts in English from Monday to Saturday on 747 MW.

Money Matters

The Euro (€) is the unit of currency used in the islands. There are seven denominations of the Euro note: € 5, € 10, € 20, € 50, € 100, € 200 and € 500; eight demoninations of coins: 1 cent, 2 cents, 5 cents, 10 cents, 20 cents, 50 cents, and € 1 and € 2. There is no limit to the amount of money you may bring onto the islands, but you are not allowed to take out more than 3,000 Euros.

Banks are open weekdays 9am to 2pm, 9am to 1pm on Saturdays (closed on Saturdays from 1 June to 31 October). A commission is always charged for changing money, and you will need your passport. Outside banking hours many travel agents and various *bureaux de change* (look for the *cambio* sign) will exchange money, but always at a lower rate than the bank. Even if the rates on display seem attractive, the deductions which they fail to advertise will cost you dearly (tourist shops are the worst culprits). Most hotels will also change money.

If you need to transfer money quickly, you can use the MoneyGram℠ Money Transfer service. For more details in the UK, telephone *Freephone 0800 897198.*

Opening Hours

Shops are open Monday to Saturday, 9am–1pm and 4pm or 5pm to 7pm or 8pm (chemists usually close on Saturday afternoon except for the one duty chemist in each area, which is open for 24 hours). Aside from major tourist resorts, shops are closed on Sunday. Museum opening hours are variable; some close on Sunday, others on a Monday (or another weekday), while some remain open all week. Church hours also vary, but they are sure to be open for morning or evening services.

Places of Worship

Catholic Mass is celebrated in various languages in the major resorts throughout the islands (details from the tourist office, the local newspapers, or on church notice boards).

There are Anglican churches at Ciudad Jardín, Las Palmas (Calle Brasil/Rafael Ramirez) on Gran Canaria; Nuestra Señora de Carmen church at the old town harbour, Puerto del Carmen on Lanzarote. On Tenerife, Protestant services are held in the Anglican church at Taoro Park, Puerto de la Cruz, the church on the Plaza de los Patos in Santa Cruz, the Casa Sueca in Los Cristianos, and in the Pueblo Canario in Playa de las Américas. The Ecumenical Church in Playa del Inglés (Gran Canaria) is used by several denominations.

There is a synagogue in Calle Remedios, Las Palmas. Evangelical services take place on Tenerife at Hotel Andreas, Los Cristianos, and the Evangelical Church on Calle Iriarte, Puerto de la Cruz.

Police

Police responsibilities are split between the Policía Municipal (blue uniform and cap) who direct traffic and have other municipal duties; the Policía Nacional (brown uniform and beret) who are in charge of crime in the towns; the Guardia Civil (pea-green uniform and cap) who look after crime and patrol the highways in rural areas.

Postal Services

Post offices are open weekdays 9am to 2pm and 9am to 1pm on Saturday. There are no telephones in post offices but you can send a telegram from larger branches, or dictate one by telephone: *222000*.

Stamps (*sellos* or *timbres*) can also be bought at tobacconists, and from most shops which sell postcards. Postboxes are painted yellow. Use the slot marked *extranjeros* (foreign) for postcards home.

Public Holidays

1 January New Year's Day
6 January Epiphany
1 May Labour Day
15 August Assumption
12 October Columbus Day
1 November All Saints' Day
6 December Constitution Day
8 December Immaculate Conception
25 December Christmas Day
Moveable feasts are Maundy Thursday and Good Friday. In addition to these, there are several local feast days.

Public Transport
Air

Binter airlines, a subsidiary of the national airline, Iberia (*tel: London (020)*

7830 0011), runs regular flights between the islands. These are punctual and all flights are around 30 minutes. Enquire at any airport for a timetable or contact the local Binter offices at: Gran Canaria (*tel: (928) 579539*); Fuerteventura (*tel: (928) 860526*); Lanzarote (*tel: (928) 803485*); Los Rodeos on Tenerife (*tel: (922) 635958*); La Palma (*tel: (922) 426170*).

Ferries

Ferries run to all the islands, and hydrofoils or jetfoils run between Tenerife and La Gomera, Gran Canaria and Tenerife, and between both Tenerife and Gran Canaria to Fuerteventura. The main ferry operator is: **Compañía Trasmediterránea**, with offices in: Arrecife, Lanzarote (*tel: (928) 811188/*

The Catholic church of Iglesia San Francisco, Santa Cruz de Tenerife

824930); Las Palmas, Gran Canaria
(*tel: (928) 474100/474474; fax: (928)
463328*); Puerto del Rosario,
Fuerteventura (*tel: (928) 850877/
850095; fax: (928) 852476*); also **Jet Foil**
(*tel: (928) 273884*); Santa Cruz, Tenerife
(*tel: (922) 277200; fax: (922) 842244);
Los Cristianos, Tenerife (tel: (922)
796178; fax: (922) 796179*); Santa Cruz,
La Palma (*tel: (922) 411606; fax: (922)
413953*); San Sebastián, La Gomera
(*tel: (922) 871324; fax: (922) 871324*);
Morrojable, Fuerteventura (*tel: (928)
540250; fax: (922) 540250*). The
Trasmediterránea agent in Britain
is **Southern Ferries**, 179 Piccadilly,
London W1V 9DB (*tel: (01207) 491
4968; fax: (01207) 491 3502*).

Other ferry companies are: **Fred
Olsen:** Head Office: Santa Cruz, Tenerife
(*tel: (922) 628231; fax: (922) 628253*);
Las Palmas, Gran Canaria (*tel: (928)
495040*); Agaete, Gran Canaria (*tel:
(928) 228186*); Playa Blanca, Lanzarote
(*tel: (928) 517301*); Corralejo,
Fuerteventura (*tel: (928) 535090; email:
fredolsen.es; www.fredolsen.es*).

Naviera Armas: Las Palmas, Gran
Canaria (*tel: (928) 474080/267700*);
Arrecife, Lanzarote (*tel: (928) 811037*);
Playa Blanca, Lanzarote (*tel: (928)
517912/13*); Puerto del Rosario,
Fuerteventura (*tel: (928) 851542*);
Corralejo, Fuertaventura (*tel: (928)
867080*); Santa Cruz, Tenerife (*tel: (922)
534052; www.naviera-armas.com*).

Buses
Bus services (buses are known as
guaguas) on Gran Canaria and
Tenerife are fast and reliable. The
smaller islands are less well served. If
you intend travelling a lot on buses,
consider a *bono* (literally, voucher)
which for a reasonable annual amount
entitles you to buy tickets at about 30
per cent less (available from main bus
stations). Central bus station telephone
numbers are as follows: Gran Canaria
(*tel: (928) 368335); La Gomera (tel:
(922) 219033, 219244/219055/219099);
La Palma (tel: (922) 411924/414441/
420060); Tenerife, Playa de Las Américas
(tel: (922) 795427*), and Puerto de la

The 'Won't-take-no-for-an-answer' attitude of some time-share touts can be frustrating

Cruz (*tel: (922) 381807);* Fuerteventura (*tel: (928) 850951);* and Lanzarote (*tel: (928) 811546/812458).*

Taxis

These are recognisable by a green light in the windscreen or on a white roof and an official plate with the letters SP, standing for *servicio público* (public service). The light shows *libre* (free) when they are available for hire. For short trips within tourist areas many cabbies won't bother to put their meters on, though you will rarely be cheated. Boards by the main taxi ranks display fixed prices between the most popular destinations. For longer distances confirm the price before you start.

Senior Citizens

Senior citizens are well catered for by many hotels on Gran Canaria, Tenerife, and, to a lesser extent, Lanzarote, by specific styles of holidays and long-stay discounts.

Students and Youth Travel

For various reasons the Canary Islands do not attract the back-packing youngsters seen in many other holiday islands throughout the world. There are some official camping sites and few youth hostels.

Telephones

You can now make international calls from virtually any phone on the islands. The best way to phone home is from a telefónica cabin, which comprises metered booths where you pay after your call. This is not much more expensive than a street phone and you

don't need mountains of change to hand. The LED indicator above your phone is not the amount in Euros you are spending, but the unit charge (which is considerably less). Telefónicas are generally in central locations and open late. Hotels usually levy a hefty surcharge. Calls are cheaper after 8pm.

For international calls, dial 00, wait for the tone to indicate that you have a line, then dial your country code (Australia 61, Canada and the USA 1, Ireland 353, UK 44), followed by the local code (omitting the first 0), then the number.

All the Canary Islands' telephone numbers now consist of nine digits. Those within the province of Las Palmas (Gran Canaria, Fuerteventura, and Lanzarote) start with (928), and those within the Santa Cruz de Tenerife province (Tenerife, La Gomera, La Palma, and El Hierro) begin with (922). The nine digits must be dialled for all calls, including local ones.

The Thomas Cook Network Licensee in the Canary Islands is Ultramar Express with locations at: Luis Morote 37, Las Palmas, Gran Canaria (*tel: (928) 273022);* Plaza San Bernardo 17, Las Palmas, Gran Canaria (*tel: (928) 367455);* Avenida Galdar SN, Maspalomas, Gran Canaria (*tel: (928) 761193);* La Hoya 26, Puerto de la Cruz, Tenerife (*tel: (922) 388715; fax: (922) 384924);* Callao de Lima 70, Santa Cruz, Tenerife (*tel: (922) 246362).* These locations can offer emergency assistance in the case of loss or theft of Thomas Cook Travellers' Cheques.

Thomas Cook's website, at *www.thomascook.com* provides up-to-the-minute details of Thomas Cook's travel and foreign money services.

Time

The Canaries maintain Greenwich Mean Time in the winter, which is one hour behind most European countries and in line with the UK. The clocks go back one hour in summer. The Canaries are five hours ahead of US Eastern Standard Time, and eight hours ahead of Pacific Time. Johannesburg is ahead by one hour, Australia by 10 hours, and New Zealand by 12 hours.

Tipping

Most hotels and some restaurant bills include a service charge. A small tip (around 10 per cent) for a well-served meal, a friendly taxi driver, or hotel staff who have been particularly helpful, will be appreciated. Don't forget to leave the hotel maid something, too.

Toilets

Public toilets are very clean and recommendable, with beach areas having in most cases a public (free) shower on the beach, and private showers/toilet facilities for a small fee. In order of preference, use those in hotels, restaurants, and bars. Buy a drink in the latter as a matter of courtesy.

There are several terms for toilets: *servicios*, *aseos*, WC, *retretes*. The doors are usually marked *Señoras* (ladies) and *Caballeros* (gentlemen).

Tourist Information

All the islands have a central tourist office (*turismo*) and the larger resorts have their own town offices (listed in **What to See** under the appropriate locations). Free maps and leaflets are usually on offer together with bus timetables (not to be taken away) and sometimes other 'what's on' lists. All offices have at least one English-speaking member of staff but the service you get depends very much on which member of staff, you see. All offices should be able to help you with accommodation.

Before leaving home, contact your Spanish National Tourist Office:
United Kingdom 22–23 Manchester Square, London W1M 5AP (*tel: (020) 7486 8077*).
USA 665 Fifth Avenue, New York, NY 10103 (*tel: (212) 759 88 22*).
Canada 2 Bloor Street West, 14th Floor, Toronto, Ontario M5S 1M8 (*tel: (416) 961 3131*)

Calling home has never been easier

The versatility of tiles in Santa Cruz de Tenerife

Australia 203 Castlereagh Street, Level 2–Suite 21a, PO Box 675, 2000 Sydney NSW (*tel: (61) 2 264 7966*).

Travellers with Disabilities

There are wheelchair facilities at all the international terminals, and as hotels and apartments continue to be built, so more choice becomes available for the wheelchair user.

Most of the wheelchair-equipped places to stay are in the newer resorts of Playa del Inglés on Gran Canaria, and Playa de las Américas on Tenerife. Another possibility is Puerto de la Cruz, which offers several wheelchair-friendly hotels. (For wheelchair hire, *tel: (922) 750540.*)

There are two purpose-built centres on the islands for the disabled holidaymaker. On Tenerife in Los Cristianos is the Mar y Sol resort. (For direct information *tel: (922) 750540*; for information from the UK, contact: ATS Travel, 1 Tankhill Road, Purfleet, Essex *tel: (01708) 863198*). On Lanzarote in Puerto del Carmen is Casas Heddy, a Norwegian-inspired enterprise. (For

details and bookings, write to: *Postboks 3083, Elisenberg 0207, Oslo 2, Norway.*)

General facilities throughout the islands are poor to non-existent. There are very few adapted toilets, no adapted public transport facilities, or adapted hire cars (even automatics are rare). Kerbs are high and the terrain is steep.

The Spanish association for disabled travellers is Federation ECOM, Gran Vía de las Corts Catalanes 562-2a, 08011, Barcelona (*tel: (3) 217 38 82*). UK travellers should contact the Holiday Care Service for their special fact sheets on Gran Canaria, Lanzarote, and Tenerife, and for any general advice: 2, Old Bank Chambers, Station Road, Horley, Surrey, RH6 9HW (*tel: (01293) 774535*).

Santa Cruz de Tenerife tile sign

ACKNOWLEDGEMENTS

Thomas Cook wishes to thank the photographers, picture libraries, and other organisations for the loan of the photographs reproduced in this book, to whom copyright in the photographs belongs.

MARY EVANS PICTURE LIBRARY 134
PICTURE COLOUR LIBRARY 18, 39, 41, 42, 50, 62, 77a, 84, 116, 118a, 121, 128, 130a, 130b, 133, 141, 145, 149
SPECTRUM COLOUR LIBRARY 3, 16, 19, 20, 21a, 21b

The remaining pictures are held in the AA PHOTO LIBRARY and were taken by CLIVE SAWYER.

FOR LABURNUM TECHNOLOGIES

Design Director	Alpana Khare	**Photo Editor**	Radhika Singh
Series Director	Razia Grover	**DTP Designers**	Neeraj Aggarwal,
Editors	Madhavi Singh, Rajeev Jairam, Deepshikha Singh		Harish Aggarwal

Updating and additional research on this edition was done by Hilda Ann Smith.

Travellers

Feedback Form

Please help us improve future editions by taking part in our reader survey. Every returned form will be acknowledged. To show our appreciation we will send you a voucher entitling you to £1 off your next *Travellers* guide or any other Thomas Cook guidebook ordered direct from Thomas Cook Publishing. Just take a few minutes to complete and return this form to us.

We'd also be glad to hear of your comments, updates or recommendations on places we cover or you think that we ought to cover.

1. Which *Travellers* guide did you purchase?

_____

2. Have you purchased other *Travellers* guides in the series?

Yes ☐

No ☐

If Yes, please specify_____

3. Which of the following tempted you into buying your *Travellers* guide:
(Please tick as many as appropriate)

The price ☐

The FREE weblinks CD ☐

The cover ☐

The content ☐

Other_____

4. What do you think of :

a) the cover design? _____

b) the design and layout styles within the book?_____

c) the FREE weblinks CD?_____

5. Please tell us about any features that in your opinion could be changed, improved or added in future editions of the book or CD:

_____

_____

Your age category: ☐ under 21 ☐ 21-30 ☐ 31-40 ☐ 41-50 ☐ 51+

Mr/Mrs/Miss/Ms/Other

Surname_____ Initials_____

Full address: (Please include postal or zip code)_____

_____

Daytime telephone number: _____

Email address: _____

☐ Please tick here if you would be willing to participate in further customer surveys.

☐ Please tick here if you would like to receive information on new titles or special offers from Thomas Cook Publishing (please note we never give your details to third party companies).

Please detach this page and send it to: **The Editor, Travellers, Thomas Cook Publishing, PO Box 227, The Thomas Cook Business Park, Peterborough PE3 8XX, United Kingdom.**

tear along the perforation

The Editor, Travellers
Thomas Cook Publishing
PO Box 227
The Thomas Cook Business Park
Peterborough, PE3 8XX
United Kingdom